T <!-- partial --> and

Don Quincy de la Mangement

Michel D. Cervésasse

ISBN-13:
978-1461085553

ISBN-10:
1461085551

"Dickens, Melville, Flaubert, Dostoevsky, Joyce,
Garcia Marquez … now this thing."

Cervantes

Bill
Hope it makes you
Smile
Wm Bro Ryan
9/2012

CONTENTS

Author's Preface and Dedication

PART I

PART II

AUTHOR'S PREFACE

AND

DEDICATION

*I*dle reader: and with "Idle" I mean no insult, but rather to suggest with the utmost civility that this book is best read when the reader is idle and disconnected from any other activity. For it is of a different sort, and its reading demands much tolerance and persistence.

This failing has placed me in great cogitation and abstraction, and I have often resolved that my most noble friend Don Quincy should be buried and not shared beyond the poor boundaries of my own computer screen. I am by nature shy and ashamed of my shallowness and want of learning, and this attempt to follow the work of a great writer of the ages is an act that, I am sure, will be seen by those who find their life's worth in the study of that author more as a slur than as a tribute and more as a theft than as an endeavor to address and enlighten another arena.

To the purveyors of new public management theories and ideologies, my hero is an injury, a challenge and an unwelcome test. And Don Quincy's most natural allies in the realm of the witty drawing arts may not see nor recognize the merit of his prose-like form. Lastly, in spite of my most honorable intentions, innocents in government, who might otherwise be a support, may think they recognize themselves in the story and regard Don Quincy and his assistant Sondra Pantolini with affront.

Still, dearest reader, in anticipation of your earnest interest and kinship, I did, almost with tears in my eyes, so desire to present this work to thee freely, plain and unadorned by the testimony and endorsement that would comfort those who instruct in public management and those who profess love for the imagination and thought of that great writer.

But to leave it bare of such support would carry daunting financial risk and could see this work go unrewarded for any good thou mayest think of it.

One time, as I thought these thoughts with my face down on my keyboard, my lively and clever wife, lady mine, my Dulcinea, entered the room and asked the reason I and my computer had been so quiet. To which I, who keeps no random thought secret from her, said I was attempting to write the requisite Preface to the story of Don Quincy de la Mangement, but for reasons already explained, I was filled with doubt.

Hearing this, my wife, gave herself a slap on the forehead and me a hug.

"Don't be so serious. Do you think Cervantes had no sense of humor ? Do you think he would not be amused by this?" she exclaimed. "After all, he worked for the government too, and it got him thrown into prison: twice!!"

My wife challenged me to look to my model for the answers to my dilemmas, which are the same, she said, as those that have troubled writers in other formats since 1605.

"Cervantes himself talked about making up quotes and testimonials from imaginary people like Prester John of the Indies or dead ones like the Emperor of Trebizond," she said. "You could do something like that too. Just don't take your made-up reviews and quotes seriously yourself; besides didn't the American Library Association call you a master of 'purple prose' anyways? That would be a good thing here."

But I explained that none of these thoughts would erase my shame over having stolen from such a great and talented personage. I then noted that literary critics have called him a genius and the font of all modern literature and that Harold Bloom, for one, said that only Shakespeare comes close to his talent and that Shakespeare would have to wrap all of his best plays into a single folio to match Don Quixote. Other evidence I offered included the Norwegian Nobel Institute's almost recent book club survey of the world's leading authors, who collectively chose Don Quixote as the best novel of all time. Cervantes' biographer Jean Canavaggio, I quoted, said his literary debtors run "From Dickens to Melville, from Flaubert to Dostoevsky, from Joyce to Garcia Marquez."

"Well, basically you're saying everyone tries to emulate his style, so why fuss about it," my always wise wife replied. "Just make it a mission to do things to promote Don Quixote and Cervantes as your penance and get on with it."

These thoughts did much to reduce my diffidence and order the chaos of perplexity that surrounded me. Still, what came next was advice that not only broke down and crushed more of the obstacles before me but comforted me to the farthest rims of my imagination.

"Look, everyone knows a hundred guys like Don Quincy and a thousand men and women like Sondra Pantolini," my wife said with unequalled intrepidness. "Anyway, everyone is going to think that you were writing about yourself so just tell them that I was the model for Sondra."

Because my lady is the person least like this character, I could not accept this munificent suggestion and debated.

"Do whatever you want," my wife said, changing the question. "It was just an offer, you don't have to take it, but

I do know that I can help you solve your problem about money and still allow you to give the story away."

She had my interest with even greater power.

"Do like Cervantes; take a loss on Part I and see if anyone likes it. Then issue it again along with a Part II for sale as a package," she elaborated. "You run the risk of someone copying your work and losing out to imitators in the short term; but you said that your real goal was to disrupt public management ideologies so you should be happy if you are ripped off and plagiarized on Part I, just keep the meatier Part II in reserve."

In profound silence I listened to my wife and reflected on what she had said, and her observations made such an impression on me that, without attempting to question them, I admitted their soundness, and out of them I determined to make this Preface.

But my wife's good sense and my good fortune in finding such a partner in life became most apparent in her final comment to me that night. It was one that rolled all my concerns and the issue of reward financial into a single stroke.

"If you remember, Cervantes did not pick the dedication for Don Quixote lightly; he used it 'strategically' as your hero would say," my wife said in closing. "Cervantes dedicated his book to some prince or duke who was in a position to help promote the book and probably to direct some money toward its publication and distribution."

So advised and counseled, I thus present the story of *The Life and Adventures of the most Strategic, Integrated and Aligned Servant of the Public Don Quincy de la Mangement.*

☼☼☼☼☼☼☼☼

DEDICATION

To the Unequalled, Peerless Princess of all that is Virtuous
and Most Popular – OPRAH – and the Good People Who
Collectively Comprised and Constituted her Book Club.

*In the belief that the good reception and honors that you have
bestowed on books of all sorts, as a princess having had a Book Club so
inclined to favor good arts, chiefly those who by their nobleness do not
submit to the service and bribery of the vulgar, I have determined to
bring forth "The Life and Adventures of the most Strategic, Integrated,
and Aligned Servant of the Public: Don Quincy de la Mangement" in
the shelter of Your Excellency's glamorous name, to whom, we owe such
grandeur.*

*I pray to receive it agreeably under your protection, so that in this
shadow, though deprived of that precious ornament of elegance and
erudition, it will still stand as a worthy work.*

Michel D. Cervésasse
23 April 2011

Imaginary Reviews

A must-read for anyone interested in public policy, management studies, classic Spanish literature, and wedding showers."
Adam de Gaulle
Professor of Public Management

"Funny as Hell … but also a little sad."
John Prestor
The Indies News

"It makes a classic relevant to the irrelevant."
George M. Komnenos
Trebizond Review

CHAPTER I

THE QUALITY AND MANNER OF THE PRIOR WORK LIFE OF DONALD Q. BICKLE

In a federal government building, the name of which I do not care to recall, there sat, not long ago, one of those old fashioned civil servants. He was placed on the tenth floor near the elevator in an office containing a coat rack, a mat for outdoor shoes, and a desk supporting several trays: one marked for incoming memos and correspondence, another for those intended to go out, one for pencils and paper clips, and a fourth, smaller one, for unspecified "odds and ends."

Each day, he arrived at his office early with a thermos of coffee, a wrapped sandwich of ingredients not prone to decay, and a newspaper of national and international partiality. He left each evening as darkness spilled into the other offices and into the hallways of his center town building. His ritual contacts with others were limited to those with the cleaning woman who vacuumed his office fortnightly, with his late sister's daughter working as a part-time intern in Accounts Payable, and with the boy in the market who sold the newspaper that he would buy on his walk to work.

A thin, plain man of around fifty years of age, he dressed in brown or grey, occasionally dark grey, jackets with vigilantly matched ties and separate, but appropriate pants. There was little to distinguish him or to proclaim his office with the exception of the fading name plaque by his door, which trumpeted the presence of "Donald Q. Bickle, Secretary, Sector-specific Programs Advisory Board."

The original "Q" had been affixed apart from other letters. Unsecured, it fell off sometime during the first year of Donald's occupation of the office and had been replaced. Now, slightly less faded than the other letters, it stood out, drawing attention and prompting passersby to speculate "Quentin" or "Quincy" or "Quiche." As will become apparent later in this account of his life, the most reasonable conjecture now seems to be "Quincy," but this is of minor importance to the gentleman's tale.

Once each month or so, more often, it seemed, around the change of seasons, someone new to the building would say quite boldly and very close to his door, words that were almost precisely the following: "This is a Q. Bickle? It sure looks like an 'office' to me." Then they would laugh and walk on.

On a particular late fall day, the in-box on the desk of the office of Donald Q. Bickle, Secretary, Sector-specific Programs Advisory Board, received a 7.5 inch by 10.5 inch cardboard calendar projecting the pay days, holidays, and similarly important-to-the-operation-of-government dates reaching out over the following twenty-six month period. The piece of cardboard covered the last two months of the present calendar year and the full twelve months of the following two.

As he pulled the old washed-out calendar (the one that he had received in like fashion two years earlier) to replace it with the new one under the clear plastic skin on his desk cover, it occurred to Donald that his Board had not met during this entire preceding two-year period and for some time before that. The workload of the Sector-specific Programs Advisory Board had been dwindling almost from its inception several decades earlier, and now Donald had to ask himself "has it completely dried up ?"

Conceived as a means of rationalizing the infrastructure of advice to government, the Advisory Board was established on the assumption that the government could more efficiently manage advice from private sector and other non-federal experts and observers if they were pulled together into a single, less annoying body. It would work better, it was said, than the unseemly mélange of meaningful and useful government advisory committees.

At the time, the government was burdened with the administrative expense and policy coordination costs of maintaining such bodies for each of some twenty peculiar government programs targeted on salvaging, supporting, and stimulating a specific industrial sector. Each had been deemed at one time or another as being of vital national importance. Formally, they remained so, but not quite so vital or so important as to merit specific, informed, and regular guidance any longer.

At times, a sector-specific program and its associated advisory committee were established in response to an economic crisis in a certain industry, other times thoughtful projections of international trends prompted wise government to proactively intervene in a specific industrial sector, and other times a sector chanced to concentrate itself in a region of specific political interest.

On occasion, the managers of particular government branches, sections or strategy teams merely thought it would be nice to have identified groupings in the private sector with the same names as their government programs, and they set about developing services aligned with the imagined industrial sectors

Notwithstanding their eclectic origins, this lightly allied array of advisory committees had the advantage of embracing expertise and interests knowledgeable in the technical and business issues of the individual sectors, and they served their programs well. But the committees were, as noted, costly in many ways. Not only did each require its own administrative and meeting support expenditures including the travel costs of committee members, but they also had the effect of amplifying the impact, effectiveness, and thus the popularity of each program's services by giving voice to the common and coordinated interests of the sector concerned. Tragically and perturbingly, they were working.

It was with this background and apprehension that a federal review of programs recommended consolidating all advisory committees into a single Advisory Board that would include high-level, "strategic" representation of all sectors and well motivated non-experts, to thereby provide, as the government had announced, "a powerful national forum to identify common issues of concern and to reconcile priorities" – and as it was explained privately, "to keep each industrial sector off guard and each pressure contained."

This model of an integrated, strategic-level, pan-economy Advisory Board had been conceived by the senior department of the Treasury official who had managed that comprehensive, multi-year review of federal programs. This man had been rewarded for his innovative public management thinking, his ethical leadership, and the specific program reviewing task with an appointment to a powerful position atop one of the operational departments. It was the one that he himself had identified with great integrity as "needing new leadership" in his report. It was the government organization responsible for oceans, coastal protection, and, significant to this tale, salted fish.

From this new post, the powerful and creative man sought to ensure the implementation of his innovative-and-sure-to-be-award-winning, integrated Advisory Board design by directing his oceans and coasts managers to reassign administrative support from this department's sector-specific programs and advisory committees to assist and encourage the department for commerce and industrial development in the creation of the new potentially award-winning body.

It was thus that Donald Q. Bickle, policy advisor and administrative officer to the Salted Fish Industry Advisory Committee, was elevated from three levels below the executive class to two levels below and to his career defining appointment as Secretary to the nationally mandated, integrated, pan-government Sector-specific Programs Advisory Board.

He would be physically located and administratively supported in the department for commerce, but reporting in a human resources way to the Director General, Oceans, Water Pollution, and Harbor Dredging, in the other department as this other one had transferred Donald and the money to cover Donald's salary in his new responsibilities.

In the first years in this newly created position, Donald was quite busy. He had to ensure the biographical information was collected, collated, and condensed to assist senior officials in many departments and eventually political decision makers in selecting and appointing the Chair and other members of the Board. Later, he worked intimately, in a professional sense, with the Chair, a man whom Donald knew well as having been a former Chair of the Salted Fish

Industry Advisory Committee in Don's old and quasi-current department.

The Chair was an affable and esteemed one-time businessman whose political connections were just strong enough to offset concerns among officials, who noted his "energetic business and personal life and past difficulties in any roles that called for bridge-building and consensus-making."

Nevertheless, the Chair was appreciative of the call to duty that this task represented, and he kept Donald busy with questions about government policies and procedures, expense claims food allowances, and travel arrangements for many months. Similar, but less demanding, support was required by the twenty other members of the Board. They each either represented an industrial sector served by one of the twenty sector-specific government programs or had been appointed because of their independence and lack of first-hand knowledge of any of the issues or matters expected to come before the Board. The Board was to meet up to three times per year.

Members would not receive any remuneration save for travel costs and other expenses resulting from meeting participation. Perhaps, the Board was predestined to see its realm diminish with time. As Donald and many other government officials knew well, sector-specific programs are, due to their essential character, ephemeral creatures. They often fade away with the passing of the political and policy pressures that spawned them, usually to manifest as tax credits with catchy acronyms or other new forms and under new names shortly after. These programs also made excellent targets for sacrifice in the era of trade liberalization and consequent agreements to prevent sector subsidies.

Over the years, in an ostensibly systematic, albeit uncoordinated fashion, each one of the programs that constituted the founding family of twenty sector-specific programs in the Advisory Board's portfolio disappeared. The pot was not replenished with new programs or replacement services. The architects of any new replacement programs wanted to avoid the damning brand of "sector-specificity" and presented themselves now as broader efforts to encourage innovation, sustainable development, or regional interests.

At the same time and independently, few government and industry officials lusted for the "constipation and confusion" that became recognized as the hallmark of the Board by those touched by its unfocused and complicating, hydra-like "advice." Most swore to avoid it at all cost in future endeavors. New programs preferred instead to have their own advisory committees and expert advice from individuals who were actually expert and interested in the germane issues.

It was thus that the point came at which the Sector-specific Programs Advisory Board had little or nothing to meet about, and no one seemed to care that it continued to exist on paper as a withered and dry, but benign appendage on the body of government. Donald Q. Bickle was forgotten in the course of events, settled as he was between programs, departments, budgets, and accountabilities.

The decline and disappearance of actual job-related work was so gradual and seemingly natural, it even went unnoticed by Donald himself. At first, he saw his challenge as preparing more focused agendas and plans for unlikely Board meetings and for the possibility of in-depth discussions around issues affecting the smaller portfolio. The Board Chair seemed to agree that this would be a good approach or, at least, never dissuaded it in his periodic phone conversations about expense claims with Donald.

Comforted, Donald had thus made it part of his daily routine to purchase that nationally oriented newspaper on the way to work, to read it thoroughly and thoughtfully each morning, and to incorporate the information into his after lunch practice of assessing the state of the sectors formerly served by the original programs under the Board's purview in order to better anticipate a call for a meeting or a request for information from inside or outside the government on Board functioning.

Those who noticed Donald's presence in the building or read his name plate assumed that he was receiving direction and was being tasked by the Board and the implicit multiple interests he served. Only one other person had any real sense of the truth in this regard. This was the Chair, whose death from histamine poisoning, almost precisely eighteen months before the commencement of this tale, had gone unnoticed and unrecorded anywhere in the Government.

Those who had recommended his appointment as Chair and had known him personally had long ago left the federal service, and the accounting systems established around his position were perpetual within the infrastructure and only required invocation to reimburse expenses not to pay a stipend or salary. The official memorandum of appointment said that the Chair's term would run "five years with an automatic renewal every five years unless it was mutually agreed that it should continue in this same manner or should not be changed in anyway whereby both parties are shown to be in agreement with continuing the appointment to its full term and will thus be terminated."

These words had led the Chair to assume that his term was up unless he had some sort of conversation with someone about something. For many years, phone calls from Donald seemed sufficient. But for a long time, well before the man's passing, Donald had nothing to call about and had left it to the Chair to determine when they would have any contact or any meetings.

For the Government's part, its processors had, however, read the same agreement and entered it into the enduring system with the assumption that it should be automatically renewed every five years and would take a deliberate act and formal written communications to terminate the appointment and instigate the search for a new Board Chair and possibly an assessment of the Board's status and affairs. There was no one with either the inclination or the interest to see that such communication would ever come.

The effect of all this on Donald Q. Bickle's working life was to see it progressively consumed by matters of a more general nature and not directly related to his formally assigned duties as Secretary to the Advisory Board. He continued the daily scan of the newspaper in his office each morning, and he continued to assess the Advisory Board implications of what he had read in the paper over the course of each afternoon.

Then as the electronic age flowed over the federal public service and its institutions, he found himself devoting an increasing amount of time to reading email messages sent to him as a named correspondent on an abundance of mailing lists. As the twenty inaugural Advisory Board programs had implicated some twelve federal departments and two federal agencies, Donald was a designated recipient of administrative email messages and notices from many, many sources at all levels in all these organizations. His receipt of these messages would be more than doubled by his accompanying duty and right to review all messages sent to the Advisory Board Chair's government email address.

The consequence of this situation was an extreme level of exposure to government administrative messaging. The impact was severe. Whenever the central government machinery seized upon a noteworthy consideration requiring the attention of all public servants such as the importance of fiscal prudence, the need for integrity in all activities, or the value of client service, Donald would read and absorb them many times.

The same flavors of public management priorities would waft across anyone with ambition and astuteness within the various agencies and departments gripping Donald's email address in their systems. These management inspired individuals would then be prompted to share comments and observations on the latest epistles from on high with their mailing list colleagues.

If alliance with a specific government priority was in vogue, Donald Q. Bickle would read the message some forty to fifty times in an assortment of different formats per day. The effect on his brain was even greater than these numbers might suggest as two such messages would be two times alignment not merely one plus one. It was an exponential drying of the brain.

Reading messages without meaning such as "our strategy seeks to be strategic," "we must not integrate merely for integration's sake, but rather embrace the inherent benefit of integration for its own worth," or "we must strive to align all of our activities with the federal alignment initiative" sapped his reasoning and his capacity to ascertain the meaning in all words, thoughts, and ideas.

It was also emotionally wearing.

He felt the exaltation of good news such as the government-wide adoption of a greater commitment to excellence, and he ached with immeasurable anxiety when seeing repeated and pervasive references to a foreboding need for "expenditure control," "adjustments," and "restructuring." Too often, these good and bad vagaries were sprinkled over single sentences in a contorting mixture that was not only impossible to decode, but irreconcilable for the heart and the soul.

The stress of such persistent mental stoning would be a test for the integrity of the strongest and most balanced personage. But it was particularly impairing for the isolated and devoted Donald who grew to make them the focus of his working life. On this day, as he sat looking at the new calendar, Donald Q. Bickle, who truly worked in an office with a door, was overcome by two potent thoughts. One thought was quite perceptive and sane. The other was the strangest, most creative, outlandishly wonderful, and imaginatively odd notion to have ever hit upon the head of a federal civil servant or perhaps upon the head of anyone anywhere.

His sane and perceptive thought was that although securely employed with compensation assured, he no longer had any work to do and absolute and unreserved liberty to define his own duties and personal mission. His strange and ensuing fancy was that it was right and requisite that he should put his unique workplace sovereignty, his profound knowledge of public management issues and priorities, and his person at the full service of his department and his country by making himself a "manager-at-large."

He immediately saw an image of himself roaming the floors of his department's head offices providing strategic advice and value-added input in all the hallways, offices, and meeting rooms. He would be acting without regard for the breaks approved in his collective agreements or the pressures of bodily functions.

Wherever and whenever a situation called for a commitment to integrity, to excellence, to service, and to the other government and organizational values deemed worthy of upholding in the most recent messages to his email address, he would act and intervene. While his own honor was not the spring of his strange notion, it quickly occurred to him that such service would not go unrewarded and that he should anticipate eternal and worldwide renown and eminence within the department and its bimonthly employee recognition program.

Donald had tasted the sweet elixir of such fame a few years earlier when the complete evaporation of Advisory Board meetings resulted in a specific, measurable, realistic, timely, and attained reduction in expenditures associated with its operations and his work.

He was commended in writing for his contributions to improvements in efficiency and provided with a certificate proclaiming same that bore national symbols, a replica of a signature, and, on the back, instructions for framing. Although never suitably framed, the certificate's adherence to his office wall was often soothing for Donald as he struggled through the troubling mass of email messages.

He was particularly buoyed when he saw the Advisory Board's cost reduction success highlighted and cited in the annual reports of three federal departments that year. As it was difficult to show improvement upon zero meetings and zero expenditures, this was to be the last such certificate of recognition he would receive.

But now, with the prospect of a new status as manager-at-large, other honors were to become routine, he was certain, and he set about devising the methods to achieve his strange and ingenious object.

CHAPTER II

THE DROLL METHOD BY WHICH DONALD WAS DUBBED A MANAGER

Having divined, defined, and devised his objective, Donald Q. Bickle set out over the following days and weeks to acquire and assemble the personal attire, the appurtenances, and trappings known to be the essentials of managers working in the civil service. Sadly, he realized that his homely, but comfortable garments would have to be placed in stores. Henceforth, he would come to work wearing a suit coat and trousers cut from the same cloth and of the same color. Donald could expect many bonuses, special rewards, and increases in salary as he moved into and up through the management class. But here at the outset of his new enterprise, he would have to remain frugal in the use of money and virtuous in matters of finance if he were to show his capability as a manager. This meant making do with the suits that he already had.

He had only one. It was a white suit featuring what some in his family had called the "dinner jacket." Its pants had a braided ribbon down the side to cover the seam. The white suit had been rented by Donald's father to attend a wedding many years ago and was eventually bequeathed to Donald for eternal care. The rented, white suit was not returned after the wedding because Donald's father had trickled wine onto the pant leg and suffered too much embarrassment to return it. Now, the unfortunate, awkwardly placed stain had faded into beige.

Donald's father and the suit were many times bigger than he, and he had to use the wide sash that came with it as a kind of cloth belt to hold the suit up and together. Donald looked daunting and unique. Just the effect that he was seeking.

He resolved to restore his white suit to its original faultless state and reduce its size someday, but for now it would meet the requirements of a novice manager with other things to attend. Wearing the same distinctive suit each day, he might have attracted stares and comments had he not arrived early and left late, spending all the time in between inside his office trying to select and install a suitable new, more managerial-like password for his computer.

Donald's ancient computer was known to the IT (Information Technology) management staff as the "Resend Antique" because of its user's proclivity for sending the same email messages over and over again to reinforce his points and as a safeguard procedure.

Now, although he was motivated in part by the fancy of giving his loyal and dependable workhorse a mantle that matched that of its owner, he was also aware that he now needed to be more attentive to such devices as passwords. He would have important management information and thinking to protect from unauthorized, untrustworthy, and unordained intrusions. He needed a strong password – one lofty, sonorous, and significant.

His old password had been his year, month, and day of birth since his first computer arrived and was installed by a technician many years earlier. As the password was entered for him, he was not sure how it could be changed. He liked his permanent and personalized password anyways, and it was a struggle to conceive of another of equal strength and association. Finally, after four days of thinking, he conceded that the dawn of his new life as a manager-at-large would be an appropriate new date-based password and would thereby tag his computer companion equally with the brand of manager-at-large, and he pulled back on the reins of the keyboard to induce the instructions and letters necessary for the change.

He clicked and tried to spur the computer into action, but for naught. None of the options and names seemed to resonate or make sense. The only discernable pattern was some bias for words beginning with the letter "s": support, start, settings, save. Then, unexpectedly, he hit upon a selection that was clearly created to specifically serve members of management in the entry and alteration of electronic files and data such as passwords – "Data File Management!" Now confident, Donald assertively and purposefully entered this space and began typing and retyping his new password over and over again to ensure it took hold.

Whenever his computer froze still, he did not abuse it, and instead found other diversions. He moved the trays on his desk, the mat on the floor, the certificate on the wall, and then he moved them back to where they had been before as he sought to find a physical manifestation of the great change that had occurred in his role and his life. Donald was busy, busier than he had been for sometime at work, but all the time, he knew that he was neglecting the most important and vital actions.

He knew that he would never be recognized as a manager without it being proclaimed in a new plaque by his office door, without it being engraved into hundreds of business cards, and without it being registered in the government electronic directory. When he finally accepted the need to act and effect these changes, Donald was shocked to learn through methodical research that there was no authentic position within any of the federal departments called "manager." There were department heads, deputy heads, directors, associate directors, directors general, deputy under secretaries, and deputy directors general. There were team leaders, section chiefs, and group leaders. But none of the human resources classification systems actually listed the title of "manager," and consequently there were no regulations and no stated requirements for the act of deeming an individual to be the authorized bearer of the title. There were, at the same time, no rules barring its use. There were many people who referred to themselves as "manager" and some seemingly officially. Donald knew of at least one use of the term that had impressed and enchanted him the very first time he heard it. It struck him immediately as something that was fitting, noble, and right. "Manager of the Secretariat."

It was inevitable that this term would return to his mind and that he would decide to apply it to his own circumstance, deeming himself to be "Manager of the Secretariat for the Sector-specific Programs Advisory Board." As soon as this thought seized him, he was prepared to describe himself as Manager of the Secretariat, should anyone have chosen to ask of his duties during those days, and he devoted hours and hours to practice drills picking up his phone again, again, and again answering "Manager's Office, Sector-specific Programs Advisory Board Secretariat."

But Donald still knew that all this would not be enough to fully establish his credentials as a manager. He went onto the department's internal website and filled out the electronic order forms requesting updated business cards and a new name plaque for his door and pushed "enter."

The next day a short man arrived at his office wanting to verify the request. He told Donald that he would not get a name plaque and cards because he had not provided enough information. Donald had only entered the job title section and nothing else: not the name, not the phone number, not the email address, and not even the room number which the short man had to trace with the help of the computer information experts in his branch. Donald explained that he desired to change nothing other than the job title.

Upon further questioning and upon confirmation that Donald was giving himself the new title and that Donald was now asking that his status as manager be corroborated in this way, the short man said he could not make the change as he did not have the authority to do this kind of thing; only to order plaques and cards.

"But my dear Sir who but you as lord of these devices would have authority to approve and ordain this title upon me," said Donald, now speaking in what he believed to be the exalted tone and gist of a manager-at-large.

"I don't know," the man said in response. "Your boss; I guess."

"But what of a man who answers only to the greater good and the broad public interest," replied Donald. "What should he do to receive his rightful due but to beseech you, the one who holds the instruments of recognition and acknowledgement in his hands. If you have the power to refuse, does it not follow that you have the power to accept, and would you be empowered with this power if you were not also trusted to make such a judgment and decree."

"You know what," said the man after listening to Donald's speech and reaching certain conclusions. "I haven't got time for this crap. The only reason I came up here was that your phone was always busy and there is something screwy going on with your email system. I just wanted to tell you that you had to fill out all of the sections in the forms or you won't get your business cards or your name plaque. That's all!"

Having thus ascertained the requisite ceremonies that had to be performed so as to have himself dubbed a manager, and so thoroughly dubbed that no one could doubt it, Donald thanked the man for having acceded to his request and proceeded to right the wrongs he had made in the electronic forms. But when he came to the line called "Name" he paused and stared at the screen. Ever since he first read a memo advising public sector managers to maintain an open and relaxed atmosphere and to engage in collaborative dialogue with peers and subordinates, he had contemplated a transformation from the starchy and sober "Donald" to the genial and communal "Don." But there were many people already using that name "Don" or "Donny" in the department. There were also "Dawns" and "Dans" that would threaten, confuse, and undermine future management-related references to "Don's take on that" or comments like "Don had better be consulted before we do anything."

He might have distinguished himself with his famous and notable "Q." There were senior managers cited as "Peter J." or "Peter T." in serious office talk of the kind he anticipated about himself. But the sting of past "Quiche" speculations still throbbed in his mind and his soul.

It was thus that he boldly and deliberately typed into the form and into his future, along with the title of "Manager of the Secretariat to the Sector-specific Programs Advisory Board," the new never-before-uttered-in-this-way but soon-to-be- widely-proclaimed name "Don Quincy" Bickle.

CHAPTER III

THE FIRST SALLY OF MANAGER-AT-LARGE DON QUINCY

So then, his office being furbished with a new plaque, his computer workstation christened anew, and he himself confirmed, Don Quincy prepared to execute his design to right wrongs, redress grievances, and discharge official duties throughout his federal department and perhaps beyond. As he considered his first steps, he felt overwhelmed by the opportunity before him and by his own limitless capacity to serve. The sense and thoughts caused him to halt at his office door immobilized. His mind churned with strategic thoughts and the broad public good, and he risked collapsing from the dizzying effect. He pulled himself out of the spiral by grasping onto the thread of a recollection. Don remembered reading a hundred times one day, a message from a particularly vigorous government manager who extolled the power of visualizing "a specific client, a specific taxpayer, a specific civilian to be served in the course of fulfilling our duties as civil servants." It allowed, the innovative manager said, for a more visceral commitment to service and a more focused effort.

Don Quincy resolved to pick one such person to hold in his thoughts and to dedicate his body and soul and to pledge his-yet-to-be-undertaken, but surely-to-be-effective good deeds to this person.

He tried to conjure the image of a woodworker or miner or fisherman upon which to focus as the person to whom he might dedicate himself and his public service, but each time he closed his eyes, concentrated, and tried to direct his thoughts only one figure would come into his mind. It was the same one that had haunted his thoughts for the past ten years. It was that of a one-time young woman who may have worked in his department and who walked to the nearby elevator regularly. He had focused on her with discretion whenever she passed his office, but she probably never knew that he did and certainly never thought of the matter if she did. Her name may have been Eva or Aldonza or Dulcinea or not. He simply called her "the Lady of his Thoughts" over the years.

Now, her image was a frustration for it would not be appropriate for a servant of the public to dedicate his client service focus to another servant of the public, and he sought to push her from his wits. But as he struggled to do so and thought of whom she may have been, he realized that she could have been merely a habitual visitor and not an employee of the department. But then if she was a visitor, she could have been visiting from her post at another federal department. But then again she may have been a former employee of this department or another department and was just visiting old friends. But then, she was not that old at that time so how would she have old friends? Still, time has passed, and she may now be unemployed and thus a non-government employee and maybe she could be a worthy client for his public service focusing after all.

These thoughts swirled into the abnormal realization that the public servants are also taxpayers, also members of the public, and also civilians who are served by civil service. And he thus seized upon the happy and exhilarating inspiration that she could now rightfully serve as "the Lady of his Client Focus." But he could not call her by that name and needed a euphemistic way of referencing her in the inevitable conversations around service improvements that would come his way as the manager to be consulted most often. So, after some search for a name which should not be out of harmony with her role, he chose "Madame Toolemonde" – a name, to his mind, common, yet significant, like his new password and the title he had already bestowed upon himself.

"We must keep Madame Toolemonde in mind as we plan this initiative," he saw himself saying in admonishment of unfocused colleagues. "These communications products will have to make sense to Madame Toolemonde if they are going to be effective."

With this the last of the preliminaries established, his mind settled and his body was engaged once more allowing him to take the first step out of his office to expose himself, his nearly pure white suit, and his new mission to the halls of this particular federal government department and the world. He headed to the elevator, entered, and as the other passengers moved away from him, he leaned over to push number 23, the top floor, where he would begin his quest for wrongs to be righted and noble acts to be implemented.

He stepped out of the elevator into a very busy office filled with open air cubicles and long tables. Dozens and dozens of people were working in front of computer screens. Few looked up, but those that did stared at him in bewilderment, not knowing what to do or what to say to the strange shape before them. Don did not address any of them and instead sallied forth down the hall to pursue his grand purpose: the search for opportunities to prove his worth by advising other managers on the requisites of their work and by participating in new and glorious initiatives.

He did not have to go far. Down the first hall, he heard a male voice in enragement and the soft snivel of a youth, presumably in distress. As he came closer, Don Quincy sensed that he was approaching an occasion to fulfill his ambitions. Outside the door, he could hear and see the older man speaking through clenched teeth.

"This is nuts. Three times this week. What kind of pervert are you," he said in a shaking voice as he scolded the youth of about twenty years of age. "I have had it. I don't care who you are related to or how you got this job."

"Sorry, I won't do it again, Man," answered the youth, snickering. "It's just so boring here."

Witnessing this exchange, Don Quincy stepped into the office and addressed the older man in an angry voice.

"Discourteous and rude," he said. "This is not the way to interact with a subordinate, however young. You are to help and support your employees in the fulfillment of their individual potential by communicating in an open, honest and forthcoming manner. You, Sir, are a manager whose performance holds opportunities for improvement."

The manager, seeing before him this bulky figure in what might be blood-stained clothes with a strange cord around his waist, was startled and felt obliged to explain himself.

Speaking meekly, he said, "Sir, this kid was hired for the summer over a mountain of qualified students because of some family connections to the political level; it's bad enough that he is lazy and stupid, smokes dope in the bathroom, and mocks the other employees," the manager said. "Now, I have caught him in the photocopy room three times touching himself; you know – in a sexual way."

Don Quincy was not impressed. "I don't care what the transgression is; your job is to address it through constructive feedback, guidance, and development against collaboratively defined commitments. Not through raised voices and abuse."

The manager thought about the value of Don Quincy's advice and how it related to the specific situation at hand, recalling all the while that the department head was interested in certain financial reports being completed and delivered to his desk within the hour. He then turned to his visitor and described a strategy for moving to another stage in their interaction.

"Get the Hell out of here before I call security, Mad Max from management or whoever you are," said the now trembling, sweating and swearing man. The youth was laughing uncontrollably and hitting his manager with a stapler.

Don Quincy was satisfied that he had successfully provided strategic advice in a difficult situation and had engaged his wit and knowledge appropriately in response to a call for his service. But as he walked away, he knew that he had other tasks to complete before his duty in this circumstance could be regarded by himself and by the history of his career as have being met. He had forms to fill and file.

Don took note of the time, the room number, and the name on the door. He made notes describing the abuse and harassment that he had witnessed, and he returned to his office to search for the policies, procedures, and documents necessary to submit a formal allegation of egregious wrongdoing to the Commissioner of Public Service Wrongdoing.

Because Don anticipated fame and renown and wide respect as a manager-at-large by the time his submission reached the Commissioner's desk, he made his allegation an anonymous one so as not to prejudice the requested investigation process. He wanted the discourteous one to have a just opportunity to explain his actions without the added burden of defending the insults heaved at a colleague manager and by extension at the full and formerly extensive portfolio of the Advisory Board on Sector-specific Programs.

Donald did not go into too much detail in his allegation submission, leaving it to the professional integrity and wrongdoing investigators to determine them. He merely outlined and reported that he had witnessed first-hand the named manager harassing a youth and that the incident involved illicit drugs and touching "in a sexual way."

Thus did the competent and enabled manager Don Quincy right that wrong, and, thoroughly satisfied with what had taken place, as he considered he had made a very happy and noble beginning in his role as manager-at-large, he left his office for the day in perfect self-content, saying to himself, "Well Madame Toolemonde, I think you should be satisfied with the tax dollars paid to me today."

Months later, Don made no association with his deeds on this day with fevered talk in the hallways about an unprecedented dismissal, scandal, and turmoil on the 23rd floor.

He saw the youth often after that incident. The young man was hired full-time in the department and reassigned to a floor closer to Don's office. Whenever they would encounter each other in the elevator or corridors, the bashful youth never spoke, and although he never formally thanked Don for the valiant intervention on that difficult day, the boy showed his gratitude with hearty laughter and beaming smiles.

Seeing a young man touched by his deeds so persistently happy was the best possible reward, of course, and one that Don and any manager-at-large would covet profoundly.

CHAPTER IV

AS THE MANAGER-AT-LARGE AND HIS MISHAPS CONTINUE

While Don Quincy's arresting white suit and jarring demeanor struck everyone in the department as discomforting and odd, these changes provoked particular responses from the two people who had known him best in his former life and role. The cleaning lady, who vacuumed fortnightly, noticed the transformations from her distinctive point of view, and she commented accordingly that he should scrub the stain on his pant leg and keep the new name plaque polished. Don's niece recognized her grandfather's tuxedo and presumed that her uncle was about to be married.

"Congratulations, Uncle Don," she said. "When did this happen?"

Don Quincy's chest swelled and his face beamed as his failed mind imagined that his niece, whom he loved dearly and whose respect he had always valued, was remarking with reference to the announcement embodied in the new "Manager of the Secretariat" plaque on the door.

"It happened, perhaps as these things often do, suddenly, just a few weeks ago," Don said. "I was not looking for it, but the opportunity and inclination struck me like a blazing bolt from the exalted. It came after I had been staring mournfully at the calendar and wondering where all the years had gone and why they had passed so quickly."

Don's niece was not accustomed to her uncle speaking this way, waxing wistfully and reflecting upon a heartfelt longing. She encouraged him to continue talking and felt moved that he was sharing his deepest feelings and being so open with her.

"I know in my core, dear niece, that I am now on the threshold of a great era," he said. "Indeed, I am certain to the depths of my soul that I am destined to be a better man from now on and to use this strength to serve the good and noble citizens of our country through previously unimagined and glorious special initiatives and strategies. To you, my sweet girl, I will confide that my power comes from a singular focus on that unique personification, that Lady of my Thoughts, the one we shall know as Madame Toolemonde. "

Don Quincy then explained his intention to devote himself to righting wrongs, redressing grievances, repairing injustices, and removing abuses while still discharging his assigned duties in a professional and competent way. His niece took this to mean that her uncle had also gotten a job in HR, but she urged him to return to the subject of his lady and their union.

"Precious daughter of my beloved sister, you too must find that special person to focus upon and to whom all your energies can be directed if you are to succeed in serving your public and in realizing your better self," Don said. "This, I believe, is the essence and the hub of my own deliverance."

Don's niece was so taken by her uncle's poetic passion that she could not help but share it with her co-workers, explaining how happy she was that her uncle had found someone special and how much she had worried about him over the years. As the story of this extraordinary and poignant love spread around the office and the building, people began to look at Don differently and more generously. His eccentricity was ascribed to being "love struck" and his attire to a man preserving his money for a wedding, gifts, and a honeymoon.

The pleasant greetings, warm smiles, and words of congratulations reinforced Don Quincy's self esteem and the suspicion that his reputation as a valued and highly aligned manager-at-large, leader-to-be was building onto itself and, in turn, strengthening the community that he believed his federal department to be. The sensation reached a crescendo a few weeks later when his niece and the women in Accounts Payable staged a surprise wedding shower for him.

For Don, the event in the boardroom next to the elevator appeared at first to be a purely spontaneous and informal affair that had manifested naturally as a belated celebration of his elevation to the manager class. He, of course, approved. But not for the personal glory it caused. Rather he saw it as a natural materialization of the healthy ongoing interactions necessary to strengthen the manager-employee relationship and to pay homage to the value of people and their positive behaviors.

When, however, Don was fitted with an outlandish headpiece and was seated in the middle of the room on a frantically decorated chair, he began feeling that the event had gone too far and that the chasteness of his humility and virtue had been threatened. This suspicion was confirmed when each of the maidens approached him in turn and presented him with brightly wrapped gifts of a very personal nature: items that could only be used in his kitchen, bedroom, or bathroom.

This was too much. He was insulted. How could they imagine that he would be bribed or otherwise enticed to accept or bestow favors. Had they not read the department's code of conduct? Do they not receive electronic reminders on the perils of conflict of interest? Did they really think he needed another toaster?

Don Quincy stood up and walked out of the room. But not before admonishing the group and, in particular, his niece for her personal complicity in the scourge as the one labeled "hostess."

"Ladies of this space, I forgive your transgression, but must provide you with this constructive feedback and observation," he said adjusting his new headpiece and wiping cake crumbs from his mouth. "You endanger your collective productivity and capacity to pursue and attain excellence in the accounting of payables by seeking affirmations of your performance and soliciting laudatory managerial appraisals through the vile method and the treachery of illicit inducement."

After he left the room, everyone stared at each other open-mouthed for a few minutes then they each picked up their unopened gifts and headed back to work. Don's niece cleaned up the food and dishes, and then, after stopping by her office, she went to the photocopy room and began printing off copies of her résumé.

CHAPTER V

OF THE ADVENTURE THAT DON QUINCY ENCOUNTERED IN ENGAGING AN ASSISTANT

Don Quincy remained in his office for the next fifteen days reflecting upon the impact that the adventure with the perfidious maidens of the payable accounting group had visited upon his still nascent managerial reputation. During this time of reflection, assessment, and strategizing, he continued to periodically reinforce his new password in the Data File Management arena, and he sought to ensure his physical state was maintained by accepting and acting upon the cleaning lady's advice on the maintenance and care of his new name plaque.

He might have stayed within the walls of his office even longer, but one morning he heard a woman crying incoherently down the hall in the Policy Development offices and could not withstand the drawing force of this siren call for help.

The source of the weeping sounds sat in a chair before a desk in the office of the Director of Planning Information and Data. She was round in figure, and with her shoulders slumped, head down, and arms limp, the woman formed a near perfect ball. The Director looked down at her in silence and with a rueful countenance sighed. Don Quincy recognized immediately that this situation was not like the adventure he had had with the discourteous supervisor of the former student intern, now Head of Communications, youth. He could see that the Director was befuddled and would benefit from a reminder that distressed employees can be encouraged through informal feedback that notes positive movement on established indicators of performance. He was also ready to propose that the woman in the chair might benefit from reminders of past successful fulfillment of commitments aligned to individual and organizational excellence. But before Don Quincy could interject and interpose advice to assist his colleague manager, the man spoke to the round, sad woman in a kind and considerate way suggesting she go back to her cubicle and forget about the issue at hand until another day.

After she left, Don Quincy introduced himself, presented his business card, shared his observations, and inquired about the problem.

"She has been here for close to twenty years doing the same job," the Director said. "Well, not exactly the same job, and that is part of the problem."

The man explained that the woman, whose name was Sondra Pantolini, had been hired to read newspapers from around the world, clip out stories of importance to the department's policy group, and to paste those clippings onto paper for photocopying and distribution to managers throughout the building. As technology advanced, her role was transformed into monitoring the internet and subscription information services and sending links along electronically by email to the interested and pampered managers. Now, the Director further explained, it appears that process can easily be automated using key words and metadata systems. There was basically no real work for her to do before, and now there would be less.

Sondra Pantolini had been chosen for the post of newspaper-scanning story clipper because she spoke many tongues: English, Spanish, Italian, French, and ones that she herself called "the gypsy" languages – and could keep an eye on foreign media as well as domestic papers. This skill revealed itself most obviously when she was under stress and her efforts to communicate mixed all of the languages and the weeping and crying into an indecipherable ball of sound to match her ball of a body.

Talking about her job and the evident lack of work always caused her stress.

Every time her Director made an attempt to raise the issue and explore options for better uses of her time, it ended the same way. Sondra would slump over with her mouth squished on her chest, sobbing and heaving, and mumbling a mix of English, Spanish, Italian, French, and something that sounded like violins, and her Director would try to calm her down, abandon the conversation, and send her back to her desk.

Now, the Director saw a ray of light around the peculiar and wonderful figure in white standing at his door.

"You, Sir, are clearly a sensitive and thoughtful person with a tremendous capacity to deal with challenging human resource management issues," the Director said seeking to engage Don by emulating his style of speaking. "Can I ask if you are yourself a manager?"

Don Quincy, admiring the perceptiveness of this fellow manager of public possessions and people, replied in the affirmative and shared the detail of his special mission to act strategically in an integrated and aligned fashion throughout all floors of the department, to right that which was not right, and to uphold the traditions and honor of the managerial profession and class.

The Director of Data and Information Planning had himself been exposed daily to mass messaging of this kind, and while he sensed that the pompous and deluded man in white might be vulnerable to deception, he was not as thrown off by Don's way of speech as other employees or visitors to the department might have been. He thus chose to accept what Don said without hesitation and instead focused on the flexibility of Don Quincy's mandate, seeing in it the seeds of a solution to his problem. He probed further and asked if Don needed any help and whether he might entertain adding an employee to his team under a special assignment. The Director said that he would be willing to cover the employee's salary from his own budget.

"As you can see, Sondra is a very dedicated and passionate person," the Director said seeking again to emulate Don's style of speaking. "I believe she weeps and hurts because she pines so deeply and sincerely for the interests of, as you call them, 'Madame Toolemonde' – the taxpayers who pay our salaries and receive our services."

He had Don at "passionate," and a handshake, honor-based deal was struck in that office that day.

If challenged directly and called to speak the truth, Don would have had to say that he did not really need any assistance nor did he feel that he ever would benefit in any way personally from this arrangement. Although all human resource management case studies and authorized descriptions of the role of public service manager inferred that a manager had, in point of fact, to have some staff to supervise and manage, Don was confident that his research of the applicable policies and directives covered the full range of human resource possibilities from the blunt and clinical challenges in classification-position numbering to the subtle and sublime distinctions between compensation planning for financial administrators and that for non-financial administrators. With such study and expertise, he never saw a need to fill out his human resource management credentials with actual human interactions or with the primitive experience of employee supervision.

This new proposed arrangement, however, was an opportunity to aid another, to guide the personal and professional development of a devoted and zealous public servant, and to align this energy with the stated priorities, objectives, and goals of the department as a whole. He had no choice, but to see the stout Sondra engaged and coupled with him in his great quest for strategic initiatives in the public interest.

The next day, Sondra's Director entered her office and before she had a chance to react, he blurted out a question.

"Sondra, do you have a minute to talk about an increase in your salary," he said, knowing that this was the one work-related subject that did not cause her to immediately recoil into her shell of foreign languages and tears. "I think that I have some good news."

"Si. Yes. Mr. Director. Sir," she said in her customary and deferential style.

Although she was perceptibly disappointed to learn that her salary was not to be instantly increased, Sondra listened attentively as the Director of Policy Information and Data described the proposition. He said that she had the opportunity to work on special assignment as the assistant to a very important and influential new manager, and while her salary and job classification level would remain the same for the time being, there was no doubt that the prestige of close association to such a man would have an impact on her aspirations for more pay and a higher level. The Director also assured her that she would not have to work very hard as her new manager was a very busy man who was on the road a lot and who was involved in strategic initiatives that were being administered and supported by the staff of other groups.

Sondra was and had been for her entire two decades of government service classified as a CLK-1 (Clerk at the first level or "Click One" as they were called). She knew that her job did not necessitate a great deal of actual work or activity on the scale delineated in the usual CLK-2 job descriptions. But she saw others coming to work in CLK-2 posts whom she regarded as much less competent than she was, and she cursed the "estúpido guberment" system that was incapable of recognizing a person's competency and potential to do a job and was instead biased toward actual jobs. Besides she thought, the government should be paying her better because her job was so boring. Now, the Director was dangling the prospect of a CLK-2 before her amidst other enticements.

The Director also lured Sondra to consider the opportunity by noting that she would finally be able to abandon the noise, exhibition, and debasement of her cubicle workstation and move into an office with a door and a lock. He did not, at that moment, emphasize the details of the arrangement as they included the understanding that she would be sharing this new office with Don Quincy Bickle and that there was no provision for another computer connection in that office. Instead, he stressed the fact that she would be given one of the surplus laptops to use in her new job. It was an old one purchased from the now defunct local supplier Dapple Associates. Mottled and spotted from rough treatment, it sat around the office for years and was known to all as the "Dapple Ass." laptop.

The Director presented Sondra with Don's imposing and impressive business card printed with the newest symbols and markings around the long and lofty job title and room number, noting that "he likes to be called 'Don Quincy' by the way."

Sondra was thrilled; she signed the assignment agreement, grabbed the "Dapple," and ran out of the office. A few minutes later, maintenance workers arrived to remove her desk, workstation, and chair. The Director sent out an email announcing her special assignment and giving anyone interested direct access to the weblinks and databases that Sondra had filtered as her essential task of recent years. The next day, a large, leafy, potted artificial fig tree arrived to fill in the empty space in Sondra's now vacant cubicle.

Sondra had kept to herself over the years and had few friends. Aside from Directors with the valor to engage with multilingual hysteria, she only recalled ever talking to one person: the short man who came to put the name plaque on her cubicle many years ago.

Wanting to share the good news of her special assignment and probable promotion, she hunted the short man down and showed him Don Quincy's business card to emphasize the enormity of this new opportunity.

The man did not recall ever meeting Sondra, but he definitely knew who Don Quincy was, and he proceeded to tell her about the odd man in the white suit, who had invented his own title and dreamed up a job that did not exist. Sondra felt the familiar flow of agitation pour through her body as she considered the possibility of having made a grave miscalculation. Her other languages rose up through her dry throat as moisture filled her eyes. The short man concluded his remarks by saying "yep, your new co-worker is a bit of a nut job, lady."

At this point, Sondra lashed out and hit the man, while stammering "No es 'worker! No es 'nut job man!', es … es … miembro de … de la mangement?"

The short man was startled, but not angry, and feeling sorry for the small round woman, he tried to pacify her with assurances that no one else knew about the falsehoods around her new boss's position and delusions. But he could not resist sharing the story of this strange encounter later on with others, always culminating the account with the soon-to-be-spread-widely climatic phrase "Don Quincy de la Mangement !"

CHAPTER VI

OF THE GOOD FORTUNE THAT THE NOBLE DON QUINCY HAD IN THE TERRIBLE AND UNDREAMT-OF INITIATIVE OF THE WINDMILLS, WITH OTHER OCCURANCES WORTHY TO BE FITLY EMAILED

On the first day of her new job as assistant to Manager-at-Large Don Quincy Bickle, Sondra Pantolini was not happy. The disturbing thoughts deposited in her head on the previous Friday by the short, name-plaque man had kept her awake all weekend. Her anxiety, which flowed from the prospect of working for a reputed madman and losing her comfortable, albeit boring old job forever, was not assuaged when she stood at the door of her new office and saw her boss-to-be at his desk struggling to tie the ribbons on his wedding-shower/new-manager's headpiece. Striving to make a good first impression, she called upon the strength of a Hercules to hold back her tears and her linguistic inclinations just to say "Good morning. Mr. Don Quincy. I am Sondra, your new assistant."

Don looked up, smiled, and tried to put her at ease saying "Welcome friend Sondra. For you are to be my friend as well as my subordinate."

He immediately launched with enthusiasm into a glory-filled description of his special mandate and quest. He so talked her over, and with such persuasions and promises, that Sondra soon started to feel the pride of association and to sense the opportunity before her. Don did not directly nor unmistakably pledge a raise in her salary and a new classification level for her job. But it was clear what he meant as he spoke of being bestowed with great rewards and exalted honors. Sondra was so enchanted with this talk that she accepted without protest word that she would have no desk, no computer connections, and no access to power, that she would have to sit in a straight back chair in the corner with poor lighting, and that she would literally have the Dapple Ass. laptop on the top of her lap.

In apologizing for the conditions, Don explained that he intended to spend most of his time out of the office, just as Sondra's old Director had predicted, roaming the building looking for new initiatives and opportunities to provide strategic input. Don said that if Sondra was not required to follow along to record his deeds in her spotted laptop, she would be free to use his desk and his desktop computer as she willed anytime he was gone from the office.

Just then, at that moment, it happened. Whether it was the morning coffee or the cabbage he had eaten the night before, something caused Don to feel the need to do what no assistant could do for him. But he knew it to be discourteous to disrupt a new employee's orientation session before a scheduled break, and so he pressed on, talking about the importance of management, leadership, and the sweet blending of the two all the while grinding his teeth, squeezing his shoulders together, and holding his stomach. Then, the building force within him burst out into noises and smells that caused Sondra to grab her ears and then her nose in succession and on impulse.

Don wrapped up his speech, concluding that "great managers must adapt to the unexpected and unfortunate and their assistants are, of course, required to do the same." He then noted that it was time for a break and headed down the hall.

Don was gone for close to three-quarters of an hour, and during that time, his new assistant took advantage of the invitation to sit at his desk and use his old computer, the one the IT people derided as the "Resend Antique." As a managerial assistant and office administrator, Sondra Pantolini was not encumbered with the most diversified set of relevant skills. But because of her years of searching the internet, filtering websites for information, and feeding management email lists, she was very accomplished at the routines of establishing passwords, registering for group emails, and gaining access to the department's varied electronic information databases. So, with her vested interest in securing her new boss's status within the management hierarchy, she set to work to see that "Mr. Don Quincy" would be copied on all emails between and for departmental executives, would be included in the electronic consultations on all important policy issues, and would be invited to all departmental and interdepartmental committee meetings at the managerial level.

She had just completed all of her work when a less anxious and less intense looking Don returned to the office. As he came through the door, he heard another sound familiar to his office walls. The chime announcing the arrival of a new email message always intrigued him, and this time he was drawn to read it by an unusual subject line stressing "Secret" and "Feedback – By Close of Business tomorrow."

The email and its attachments had been sent by a director in a federal agency responsible for economic development along the eastern coast of the country. The emailing director was offering, as a standard requirement of the approval process for such projects, the opportunity for senior officials in other federal departments and agencies with economic responsibilities to comment on a proposal for a major initiative involving federal investments in the many millions of dollars. The proposal would see the construction of the country's largest offshore wind farm. It meant the erection of two hundred wind turbines stretched over thirty miles along the eastern seaboard. One thousand megawatts of electricity, it said: enough to provide power to over half a million people. The project was to stimulate the development of a new wind turbine construction and supply chain industry making blades, towers, and equipment for the region and the country.

Don Quincy knew instantly that the issuance of his new business cards and name plaque were starting to have an impact on his stature and place within the federal government system and now his management expertise and insight were being sought out on important and weighty issues. Sondra too was pleased and read the email standing on her straight back chair and looking over her boss's shoulder.

Don turned to his assistant and scoffed.

"Vile and disgusting," said Don recalling his days at the department of oceans, coastal protection, and salted fish. "This project is clearly an attempt by the oil industry to work around the environmental assessment process and build offshore oil rigs where they are not allowed, and it must be stopped."

"But, Mr. Don Quincy, this email says that they only want to build windmills," cried Sondra fearing that her boss was about to use his privileged email access to flaunt his mental instability and undermine his assistant's job reclassification aspirations.

"Oh, simple Sondra, how naïve and inexperienced you are in the ways of public policy," Don replied. "These regional agencies are always trying to disguise their self-serving and short-sighted projects with the trappings of the national interest, sustainable development, and public good."

He told Sondra to open the Dapple laptop and take notes. Then he explained how it was the role of managers charged with higher purpose to challenge such thoughtless program and policy work and to ensure that the interests of Madame Toolemonde were put above the gluttony and avarice of the parochial.

"But in our combat with these monstrous acts, we must not debase ourselves and crouch down to their low level with overt accusations of mendaciousness," he said adding that one must presume all managers to be ignorant of lying devices and to be bound to the unstained truth. "We must adhere to the values and ethical standards of public management and found our challenges upon penetrating observations on possible conflicts with stated policy priorities and by invoking the always right and just tactic of requesting more research and study."

He told Sondra that he would not call his regional agency management colleagues "liars" and attack these monsters as camouflaged oil rigs. Instead, he would list the possible environmental concerns raised by the particular configuration of wind turbines proposed in the project, with the particular design of turbine blades, and with the proposed speed of the blade turning. Don explained to

Sondra that the more that one could associate a generalized concern and public anxiety to a specific detail, the more likely the proponents would need to do more research to respond. More research meant more time, and more time meant new opportunities to obstruct.

"It is, for example, enough to say that we know people are dying of cancer and heart disease in our country, but we are not sure what the link is to wind turbines and what the precise mechanism of this linkage is," he said. "Clearly, we need more research."

"Did you get all that down, Sondra?" he asked.

"Yes, Mr. Don Quincy," Sondra replied. "But they are just windmills."

Realizing that serious threats to human health are rarely sufficient cause to stop an initiative of particular political priority and economic benefit, he went on to list other reasons for stalling, studying, and stopping this grotesque project.

"We have a unique opportunity to establish our country at the forefront internationally in the field of opposing wind power and in the study of hypothetical issues around wind energy systems," he dictated and Sondra typed. "Our country can be the world leader in the practice of studying and researching the problems with this alternative energy option."

As compelling as these arguments seemed, Don realized that the fatal blow to the so-called "windmill" project would come by citing negative impacts on the environment. He had Sondra write down a stream of projected consequences of the proposed wind farm from the creation of a new variety of tsunami to the mass decapitation of migrating seabirds.

All this long rant was concluded with the recitation of the introduction to the national policy on sustainable economic development and placed above Don's "Manager of the Secretariat to the Sector-specific Programs Advisory Board" email signature, and Sondra then pushed "send" throwing a lance across the government and into the body of this ill-advised and dangerous project proposal.

While the summer student at the regional economic development agency, who was responsible for collating and reviewing comments received in the email consultations on the windmill project, was shocked by Don's biting reply, his managers saw it differently. They regarded the admonition to conduct more study and research as an opportunity to secure incremental funding for public opinion research, something the officials in the agency longed to do in the framework of their hopes for the region's tourism industry, which was another of the agency's mandated concerns.

As a rule, thoughtful interdepartmental feedback on plans for projects like the windmill farm development would be filed appropriately for consideration and analysis later on, perhaps during the post-mortem sometime after the wind farm had been built. But because Don Quincy's input was needed to justify the public opinion research, it was kept intact and circulated through many, many hands and with many, many drafts of proposals, forms, and eventual contracts for the public survey. It was thus in the summer of that year, thousands of tourists visiting the region were asked for their impressions of the local attractions, for their preferences with respect to accommodations in the region, for their intentions for travel in coming years, and for their views on the prospect of thousands of seabirds being decapitated by wind turbines off the region's coastline.

Media interest in the tourism survey was particularly strong and vivid that year. Television and newspaper coverage of the survey results featured images of large wind turbines and the internal operations of chicken abattoirs.

Don and Sondra had moved on to be preoccupied with other initiatives and adventures and thus missed the fall news conference announcing a long term, national moratorium on offshore wind farm development.

Had Don heard the news, he most definitely would have been gratified to hear the politicians and the heads of several government agencies speaking of the need for more study and research, the importance of protecting the environment, the challenges in sustaining the economy, and concerns related to human health including the threats of increases in cancer and heart disease.

CHAPTER VII

THE COST-RECOVERER RELATES
THE TALE OF HIS LIFE AND CAREER

While the initiative of strategic and valued input on the dishonest "Windmills Proposal" was satisfying to a point, Don Quincy recognized it as a tepid experience in contrast to the vibrant planning meetings, face-to-face consultations, and collaborative exchanges celebrated in annual reports and statements of departmental priorities.

His wits thus turned to a resumption of his quest for the truthful practice of a manager-at-large; he logged-off of Resend Antique, stood up, tightened his headpiece, adjusted his sash, and headed for the office door, bidding Sondra and the Dapple to follow him on his next sally through the department.

But when he pushed the office door to open it, it would not budge. Only by placing Sondra against it and by crouching down behind her to push, did they, through the might of two bodies thrusting in unison, dislodge the door and create enough of a fissure for the thinner and more sinewy of the two to pass through and into the hallway. The hall was filled with boxes laden with documents and labeled for shipment overseas. Don bent down to pick up a few boxes near his door and to free Sondra from captivity when he heard a voice on the opposite side of the pile call to him.

"It's okay, Sir; I'll have these cleared out of here in a minute," said a man dressed in casual clothes. "You don't need to help, just sit there and I'll do it. It's my mess."

Don accepted the proposition and sat down on one of the boxes, recognizing that the inappropriately attired man was about ten years his junior and visibly fit and hale. Sondra, anxious to be freed from Don's office, peeked through the too-narrow opening at the door.

"Do you mind telling us what this is all about while we wait for you to move these boxes away," Don asked, as was his duty and right as the most senior official present in the situation. "I am prepared to wait all day for an explanation."

"Oh, it's not important," the man said with a sigh. "But if you're willing to listen to my story, sure."

The man told Don and Sondra's nose, which was now just visible through the crack in the door, that it was his last day of work after having been with the department for fourteen years. He had come into the government service in his early twenties, right after receiving a master's degree in business administration. The man said that as a student, he had hoped to pursue a career in marketing, perhaps by selling car insurance or organizing promotions for a beer company. But, he explained, he was spurned by the insurance and beer industries which were experiencing a downturn in business as the baby boom generation headed into the age of alcohol treatment and long-established insurance relationships. It was a tough time to find any job, so the man was easily seduced by the recruiters from the commerce department who were on his campus celebrating the department's most recent strategic plan and its goal to make the department a world leader in writing public service strategic plans.

They had told the students that the department was committed to tackling emerging challenges, valuing people, and celebrating creativity – at least for the next three to five years or so. The then young man was asked by the recruiters to indicate on his application form whether he wanted a meaningful or a rewarding career or both. He checked both, which apparently was the answer that screened him in for an interview and eventually gained him a job offer.

His position was that of a junior analyst for manufacturing systems policy. The duties set out in his job description, as he understood them, required that he read all engineering journals, trade magazines, and industry reports on the department's subscription list and to, every month, consult all officials across the government with an interest in any manufacturing industry issue. He was then to prepare a comprehensive background report synthesizing the gathered information in an integrated, strategic, and aligned way and finally to summarize this information in a half-page, bullet-form memo that could be sent to the head of the department, if he ever requested it.

New to government and its aversion to specificity, the then new young employee did not recognize the significance of the qualifier "such as" before the long list of prescribed duties, and he found himself working long hours, weekends, and holidays to fulfill the requirements and keep his new job. While he did not recall ever being asked to formally submit one of those half-page reports to the department head, he soon found his background paper to be a useful reference and resource. Through his energetic monthly consultations, he built up a robust internal network and reputation within the government as a source of information on manufacturing systems and manufacturing technology advances. Soon, he was being asked for information himself, and he found it easiest to respond to requesters with the most relevant issue of his monthly manufacturing systems research paper. While the cover pages with his name and branch were usually removed, copies of these papers were often shared with senior officials, clients, and stakeholders of other departments and government agencies as well as other sections of the commerce department.

"You really should be charging people for those things," one of his colleagues once said, planting a seed that would generate the creeping vine that was to encircle his life.

The man's marketing education and instincts were rekindled by the thought, and so when his department was challenged with a directive to reduce budgets in tandem with admonishments to increase services and align with identifiable clients, he developed a comprehensive plan to convert his monthly research paper into an authoritative government report on manufacturing technology news. He knew that it could generate revenue for the department, not only through internal cost sharing with other federal agencies, but also through subscription sales to industry associations, economic development organizations, municipal governments, and domestic industry. He realized from the interest and uses of his monthly research paper that the synthesized information constituted a resource of strategic importance not only to government policy, but his entire country. All this was reflected in his proposal, which comprised an uncommon-to-his-department sense of business and marketing potential.

The man's supervisor at that time, like other managers in the department, had been struggling with the incongruity of the task of reducing services while increasing services. Some had used the opportunity of the two-headed challenge to advance requests for budget increases for special projects, hastily recast as transitions to the new higher service/lower service paradigm.

The manufacturing research paper report-for-sale proposal was thus all that the man's supervisor had to put on the table when the department held its final budget reduction and increased service Management Retreat in Las Vegas that fall. In fact, it was the only specific proposal considered at the meeting, which focused primarily on the strategic challenges posed by the issue and discussions of the invigorating impact of change on public organizations.

The following week, the man was informed of the good news. His proposal had been accepted by senior management, and as a consequence, he was to be placed on "full cost recovery."

"I wasn't really sure what that meant at the time," the man told Don and Sondra's twitching nose. "But I soon became an expert in it."

"Full cost recovery" meant that the man was now responsible for causing enough sales of his research paper to cover the cost of his salary, his benefits, his electricity use, and the soap and any paper he used in government washrooms as well as a minimum annual payment to the department to cover "overhead costs" associated with his presence in the department and the building and to reward the senior officials who had conceived of this cost-recovery initiative. He would no longer have access to telephones, photocopiers, computers, or staplers. His office was being moved to a storage room in the basement, and he was advised to bring pens, paper, and a battery-powered light to work from now on.

This package of "full cost recovery" did not initially seem like the marvelously good news his supervisor suggested.

The man was already working long hours and seven days a week to conduct all the research and consultations embedded in his job description and to write and produce the synthesis paper and point-form, never-used, but always-required report for the department head. Now, he would have to find time to write a third version of his paper, a public one that was screened and edited for the sensitive information or important public policy concerns that should be preserved for the department alone. He would also have to find time to market it and negotiate sales, to manage its layout, production, printing, and distribution, and to collect receivables and account for all transactions in accordance with a mountain of government financial management regulations and policies all without soliciting advice or help from other government officials, lest he incur other obligations to the taxpayers.

His task was complicated further by the brand of "full cost recovery" which repelled other public servants who feared an assault in the workplace by someone with something to sell or who feared the taint by association with someone not purely and uniquely pledged to unsullied service of the public good and the national interest.

Don Quincy nodded and begged the man to continue although Don felt the initial stages of offense at the implicit slight at the public good and, by extension, to the virtue of Madame Toolemonde.

The man said, however, he had one very sturdy weapon with which to combat this daunting test: the strength of a good design. It soon became evident that his idea was sound, and there was enough demand for a specialized monthly government report on manufacturing technology issues to justify its preparation and production. It also turned out that the man had the panache to excel with ease not only in his trade of marketing, but all of the other elements of this special enterprise.

As he expanded his sales contacts outside of the federal realm to the manufacturing and technology systems interests in other levels of government and the private sector, he also invigorated his networks for information and technology market intelligence. His research papers and summaries became vital resources to public policy and planning across the government and a defining input in many important investment decisions.

At the same time, because his years of research and the discipline of drafting terse reports for the department head had enhanced his writing, editing, and communications skills, he was able to produce a very entertaining and informative product for his external-to-government clients. The report became a high profile hall mark of the department's services to industry and commerce. Revenues from sales soon covered the full cost of the man's expenses and salary including the cost of time he took away from business to attend a department-wide meeting of all staff to hear the announcement that the entire senior management team would be receiving extra bonuses and individual awards of recognition for "Innovative Public Management and Leadership." They were honored for having introduced a new cost recovery initiative that was said "to exemplify the values of creativity, excellence, and service that the government holds to be fundamental." The man told Don and Sondra that while he was disappointed that his name was not mentioned in any of the congratulatory speeches, he was gratified and proud whenever the commerce department's popular and award-winning "Manufacturing Technology

Update" was cited and applauded by the employees and managers.

The man said that he was happy for his senior management and his entire department that day because he knew that they were under a lot of stress and needed some good news. He told Don and Sondra that there were rumors of more budget reductions coming at that time, and he hoped that the special bonuses for senior management and their personal awards would put the department in better stead in any budgetary reviews by the government. He did not personally fear the budget situation because, by that point, his Manufacturing Technology Update report was not only paying for itself, but, in fact, generating a net budgetary benefit to the department and the taxpayers.

"I was wrong," said the man in a shaking voice with eyes dampened. "And I still can't understand the decision or explain it to my wife and kids."

He said that the government budgetary planning directive that year was worded differently than the previous time and instead of talking about the need to reduce the cost of government operations to the taxpayers or to "reduce funding" to the department, it said merely that the department had to "reduce expenditures." This turned out to be bad news for popular and effective services that paid for themselves. If a cost-recovery program is valued by its users and in demand, volume of work increases, more money pours in from sales, more products and services are produced, the burden on the taxpayer is reduced, and yet the department increases its on-paper "expenditures."

A warm light shot across the top floor of the building the day that the senior management committee realized that the department could maintain its budgetary funding allocations and still dramatically reduce its "expenditures" if it just stopped providing the services that were so popular that users would pay for them. In fact, they now recognized that the no-net-cost-to-the-taxpayer popular and useful services had the potential to expand and increase revenue-earning expenditures and were thus a serious threat to the rest of the department – the non-popular, less obviously useful part – maybe even the non-popular, less obviously useful parts of the government as a whole.

Topping the list of useful, popular, no-cost but expenditure-involving services was, of course, the man's Manufacturing Technology Update and associated reports.

Negative reaction from the manufacturing industry and other users of the popular report to its termination was mitigated by the announcement that the government would transfer the service to the private sector. The government was confident that although the Update report was highly dependent upon access to internal government information sources and was barely profitable, a competent business would step forward to fill the gap.

A tender was drawn up and issued, but there was no submissions and no interest from any companies in taking it over. The man, the former "cost recoverer," who was now on layoff notice and heart broken that a over a decade of work and a service of great national benefit was about to be destroyed, asked if he could continue publishing the report on his own if he were to form a company, take the risk, and run it as a private sector enterprise. But he was advised by the government human resources office and its legal counsel that he risked imprisonment by making such a suggestion as it constituted a conflict of interest and an attempt to use his government position and influence to gain a personal benefit. He was sent a threatening letter and ordered to stop thinking this way.

The government reissued the contract offer to try to attract a private sector supplier, this time sweetening the pot with offers of bridge funding to transition the enterprise to non-government control and with long term guarantees of privileged access to government databases, information sources, and exclusive licenses to the intellectual property of the entire archives of the Manufacturing Technology Update, its background research papers, and its confidential reports.

Finally, a company came forward to accept the government's terms of special funding, free intellectual property, and privileged access to information. The company was based in East Asia and evidently could realize special economies by locating the Manufacturing Technology Update operations and production offshore. It was a new company, but was considered a solid enterprise and one that could be depended upon because it had strong backing as a wholly owned subsidiary of the national government in its home country.

The man told Don Quincy that this deal had been finalized with the department having transferred funds and departmental access codes to the company's office in East Asia already and that the only thing that remained was the transfer of all the archival files of information that had been edited out of past Update reports for reasons of commercial sensitivity and national interest. This was the contents of the boxes in Don Quincy's hallway and the wall that was keeping his assistant captive.

"Well, it sounds like you feel that a great injustice has been committed," Don said to the former "cost recoverer" while smiling ruefully. "Perhaps, we should file a formal allegation of wrongdoing against the whole department or the whole government."

"Gee, do you think such a thing should be done?" said the man as he lifted away more boxes finally freeing Sondra who was now covered in a blend of perspiration and tears. "I just thought it was my job to help them do this private sector thing to the best of my ability and to work hard up to the last minute of my last day even though I did not personally think the decision was for the best."

Don was being sarcastic when he implied that the department or the government could ever be culpable of doing wrong. But he had made the suggestion and now had to find an elegant way out of the awkward and perhaps dangerous situation.

"Son, please provide your home address to my assistant, and we will see what can be done," said Don Quincy waving Sondra back from her effort to head to the washroom.

The man gave Sondra a copy of his one-page résumé because it not only held his personal contact information as requested, but also because he hoped that this man who had the air of a very senior manager might have some positions open in his branch or program offices. With that, Don said goodbye and walked with Sondra and the Dapple down to the elevator, entered, and pushed down.

The doors closed, and Don turned to his assistant.

"We have no choice but to look into this 'allegation of wrongdoing against the whole department' insanity because we have pledged to do so, Sondra, but the man is delusional and government service is better off without his kind in its midst," said Don Quincy with a mix of sorrow and dread. "Watch him closely my friend – if he tries to work past official hours, this being his final day, he will be breaching security, and we will have to call the authorities and give them the man's address."

CHAPTER VIII

IN WHICH IS RELATED THE PUBLIC WEBSITE REPORT OF "THE ILL-ADVISED CURIOSITY"

After watching the security guards escort the casually dressed cost-recovery man to the exit of the building and seeing his remaining boxes sent to recycling, Don Quincy and Sondra Pantolini returned to their office to complete the dutiful and perfunctory task of confirming that one could not, in fact, submit a formal allegation of wrongdoing against the government as a whole nor against an entire federal department or agency.

At her manager's behest, Sondra mounted his chair and booted the Resend Antique into action. They roamed up and down the main government internet site looking for some phrase or link to an explicit statement to the effect that the government was not capable of wrongdoing and should therefore not be troubled with vexatious allegations or charges made in ill faith to this effect. Don was sure that such a directive must exist somewhere, it only made sense, and he felt that only by finding it could he be freed from his hasty vow to the poorly dressed delusional man with the boxes.

After exhausting all possibilities on the main government site, they followed the trail into the bumpy terrain of individual departments and agencies halting at a particularly intriguing page off the main section of the website of the department responsible for domestic revenue collection. It was what officials in the department referred to as "the Pillory Page."

The page was created in the previous months and given a high profile because the domestic revenue department had been chastised for its past failure to publicly promote and celebrate findings of wrongdoing. The department of the treasury, which was responsible for managing wrongdoing in government, had cited the chief executive of the domestic revenue department for not ensuring that all cases of wrongdoing unearthed in it were described in full and posted in a publicly available format. The executive had been reminded that the government was committed to promoting integrity and ethical practices in the public sector and to creating a positive environment for identifying more wrongdoings. For these ethical reasons, departments were responsible for publicly degrading those implicated in wrongdoing issues and for informing citizens of the processes and procedures involved in doing wrong.

The story of wrongdoing featured at the top of the "Pillory Page" was entitled "The Case of the Ill-advised Curiosity." Don Quincy, now leaning over Sondra and looking at the screen, said "the title of this report does not seem to me a bad one, and I feel an inclination to read it all aloud before we move on."

Sondra was tired of clicking, scrolling, and mousing and welcomed the rest, and she leaned back in the chair to listen and let her manager read the story to her.

"The Case of the Ill-advised Curiosity – Public Report of Wrongdoing 001, Department of Domestic Revenue," he said after clearing his throat and swallowing the result. Don then read what was on the computer screen without pause or alteration.

"This is a detailed report on the activities of two departmental employees, who were engaged in actions flowing from what has been deemed an "Ill-advised Curiosity" and is presented here for the benefit of other employees, the department's stakeholders, and inquisitive members of the general public. Although the activities which are the focus of this report took place over a two-year period, this account covers the full term of the careers of the individuals involved, consistent with the department's commitment to the ethical exposure of embarrassing information and to the integrity of its obligation to share details of all touched by or exposed to possible wrongdoing activities including, to emphasize this commitment, the guiltless and those above suspicion.

To respect the provisions of federal privacy legislation while ensuring that the individuals involved are suitably shamed, this report will refer to the two men by their surname initials. They will be cited, therefore, as Elmo S. and Larry O. hereafter. For current employees of the department seeking clarification on this point, it is noted that the two men were very close friends and colleagues known widely within the department as "the two geeks."

The two men were hired at the same time ten years ago. They had attended college together and been roommates. They were computer system designers and programmers who had belonged to the same computer club in high school and had shared video games and peripherals. In the department, they worked as a team even when they were told by supervisors to not spend so much time together. Much of their early work was service support and occasionally hardware repair. But at some point in the third or fourth year of their time in the department, Elmo S., who had had his personal identity stolen and later returned by a computer hacker, started to take a particular interest in the security mechanisms of both computers and networks. He and

60

Larry O. still spent a considerable amount of time together eating pizza and repeatedly watching a DVD of the original "Tron."

Nevertheless, Elmo S. would find some time each day to devote to his particular personal interest developing a new multi-factor user authentication technique, configuring unique packet filters, or designing circuit-level gateways specifically for the domestic revenue department's operational needs. Larry O. was vaguely aware of his friend's peculiar computer-based obsession, but did not think much of it until Elmo announced that he had integrated and aligned all of his small devices and inventions into a gigantic Godzilla-sized, COMprehensive network-wide COMputer security system – that he called "Comilla." (For illustrations, technical guides, specifications, and code for "Comilla" see Annex I in the links below). Elmo S. demonstrated "Comilla" for his manager, his manager's manager, and eventually for the senior management team of the department, which had just finished attending a computer security conference in Orlando the previous week and made a commitment to purchasing or otherwise spending money on something related to the subject as a follow-up.

Larry O. was happy for his friend when funding was allocated to develop and deploy Comilla across the department and all its services. He watched and applauded as Elmo S. received special awards and bonuses, and he clapped hardest when Elmo spoke to staff meetings about the creation, and he, Larry O., even led a team to apply the Comilla technology to income tax systems. There was no doubt in Larry's mind and in the minds of many others that Comilla was an elegant, unassailable, thing of beauty. Yet its creator, said in earlier performance appraisals and job assessments to have been "an anxiety-ridden nerd and a geek," was still unhappy.

Elmo S. confided in his friend Larry O. that even though all the world was convinced that the Comilla security system was as unassailable as it was beautiful, he himself had doubts. He said that he was sure that there must have been weaknesses that he overlooked in developing the system and that someday a disreputable "black hat" would break into her bringing disgrace to him, his department, and

Comilla forever. He told Larry O. that despite all of the great things that had happened and all of the accolades that he had received, he felt like a fraud and could not suppress the dark thoughts about Comilla and could not stifle the swelling sense that he could not rely on her, that he could not trust her so-called security system virtues, and that she was not, in fact, as "good and perfect as I thought her to be."

Larry O. was distressed to see his best friend so miserable and assured Elmo S. by sharing his own admiration for Comilla's strengths and by trying to convince Elmo to abandon his anxieties and enjoy his good fortune in being linked eternally to such a stunning and graceful security system. Elmo S. responded that he was lucky to have such a good friend as Larry and that he knew that he could confide in him and trust him with any task. Larry acknowledged that he could. With this, Elmo S. presented his lifelong friend with such a disturbing and shocking proposal that Larry O. was stunned with astonishment and filled with sadness over the clear extent of his friend's troubled mind. Larry O. recoiled and fled the pizza parlour that they were sitting in at the time.

Elmo S. had asked his friend to test the integrity of Comilla by trying to hack into her system, pierce her firewall, and position himself to conduct insalubrious acts inside. Elmo said that he thought he would never be able to rest his mind and find peace without knowing for sure that the system could withstand the entreaties and assault of a programmer and network design specialist of the highest skill. Elmo said, however, that he did not want to cause difficulty for the department and the government and could not engage someone whom he did not trust utterly and completely in the enterprise. He concluded his confession by saying that he knew of only one person in whom he could entrust this task and who also had the high level of skill and caring needed to execute it. His friend and colleague Larry O.

At first, Larry thought his friend must have been joking. Then, he realized that breaching a network security system was not an act that Elmo would ever suggest in jest. It was at this point that he had drawn back in shock and had run away.

The next day when he saw Elmo at work, he assumed that the subject would be dropped as a bad mistake and that the two men would never discuss Elmo's error of judgment again. But instead, Elmo pleaded and wailed with ever greater force claiming that life would be unbearable if this issue was not resolved in his mind. The harangue continued for days and then weeks and eventually became the only subject of conversation between the two men, and Elmo would not let up on his friend despite Larry's protests and Larry's cries that he feared for his own virtue as well as that of Comilla and the department's information technology assets. Elmo could not be dissuaded from his scheme. Finally, Elmo pulled out a most terrible and hideous weapon. He threatened to break off the long, deep, close friendship that was renowned and celebrated widely as that of "those two geeks."

Shattered, exhausted and fearing that Elmo S. might resort to soliciting a new geek friend and hacker on the Internet, Larry O. acquiesced and agreed to the ill-advised plan to satisfy the profound and aching curiosity.

"It's not enough to pretend that you tried to hack into the system," Elmo S. told his friend in receiving his pledge. "If I can't trust that you have done all in your power to crack it, I'll never be assured that it's impenetrable and that I'm deserving of the awards and honours that have come my way over the past few years."

Giving his friend his word as only a best friend can give, Larry O. left work early, picked up a bottle of ginger ale and a medium pepperoni and mushroom and headed home to begin his unfortunate task. At first, despite his pledge to do otherwise, Larry only made half-hearted attempts to break into the system, each time concluding by tapping the space bar with his thumb and saying to himself "there, I knew it couldn't be done."

Finally, in order to face his friend with the clear eyes of honest belief, he resolved to try one hundred different strategies before giving up and declaring Comilla unassailable. He called his office the next day and said that he would be taking a week's vacation, his personal day holiday, and days off in lieu of overtime pay due to him, and he sat down at the keyboard of his home computer for the odd and uncomfortable marathon he had designed.

As he tried out different strategies and was pressed to conceive of others, he continued to fail as he had anticipated. But something else happened in and around his 80th attempt. Larry found himself becoming obsessed by the sport of this challenge. He woke up the next morning passionate and enthusiastic and ready for another run at the department's network. When he reached the prescribed one hundred attempts, he kept on trying and trying and trying.

He read and re-read his text books; he searched blogs, and studied hacking techniques for many days. When he was not reading, he was hacking, when he was not doing either, he was dreaming about the challenge in his light and troubled sleep. One night, he received a phone call just before bedtime from his friend Elmo S., who was still racked with anxiety and stress over his curiosity, who could not wait to hear from Larry, and who had called to see how this hacking project had gone.

Larry O., realizing that he had been at the task for just over six weeks by that time and recognizing that he risked losing his job if he did not go back to work immediately, told his friend that he had failed, that the Comilla security system was indeed impenetrable, and that he could be at ease and confident in his work and his reputation. Elmo sighed and thanked his good friend over and over. Larry noticed instantly that Elmo's voice sounded more relaxed and, in fact, Larry felt he was talking to his old friend from high school for the first time in years. And Elmo S. slept through the night for the first time since he first seized upon his obsession.

Larry, however, had a restless night haunted by the painful and sorrow-filled prospect of withdrawing from his quest. He was also flooded by decades of memories flowing from the brief exposure to his friend's normal-sounding, stress-free voice. It was thus that Larry O. awoke at 3 A.M. to shout "I've got it!" He had solved the complex and multi-headed puzzle that was the Comilla computer network security system. Larry recognized an intricate web of connections and pathways integrating all those multi-factors, authentication techniques, configurations, packet filters, circuits, and gateways – they were all tied together by designs, codes, and systems drawing upon Elmo's life, hobbies, interests, and his friendship with Larry. Factors were organized like the toppings on a pizza, the route to school, and the agendas for computer club meetings. Passwords were anagrams of Larry's last name and birthplace, and usernames employed the same technique with Elmo's personal information. Larry O. may have been the only other person in the world who had this knowledge as well as the skill at programming. He broke into the departments systems and was overwhelmed with the ecstasy of accomplishment and power. (Complete details on the process and techniques used by Larry O. in the execution of this wrongdoing are available in the web link below marked Annex II).

Seeing Elmo relaxed and fully restored the next day, Larry could not bring himself to share the news of his hacking victory knowing it would crush his renewed old best friend for good, and he swore that he would take the secret to his grave. But Larry had become obsessed and addicted; he could not stop and continued to work at the next and the next challenge now free to roam throughout the system. He tinkered with his pay to recoup the lost six weeks of wages, gave himself a few extra days of holiday, and made minor editorial changes to his past job performance appraisals. He accessed the personal information of others out of curiosity and gave a few of the nicer people in his branch extra holidays and pay as well. This low level interference continued for a few weeks, and then, Larry escalated his attack to the income tax system. That year, just under one hundred thousand individuals received unanticipated tax refunds of just under one hundred thousand dollars each. Larry, having ascertained that one hundred thousand was the threshold established for random tax audits, was implementing a seemingly faultless plot. He bought a condo and new tires for his car."

At this point, Don Quincy stopped.

"Keep reading, Mr. Don Quincy," said Sondra. "I must know what happened next."

"That's it," said Don. "It ends right there, and rightly so, as the department of domestic revenue has completely fulfilled its prescribed obligation to report and to publicize the wrongdoing and has no requirement to say whether the architect of the wrongdoing ever endured consequences or what they might have been."

"Well, that is just stupido," said Sondra in frustration.

Putting on his coat and adjusting his headpiece, Don calmed Sondra by saying that the two of them could leave work early because they had had a productive afternoon and would be facing a demanding, day-long meeting in another department the next day. They had been invited to take part in the special working group meeting thanks to Sondra's email list work in ensuring that Don would be engaged in all manager meetings of import.

Don asked his friend and assistant to engage his "Out-of-Office" email message notice and then to call it a day. Still aggravated by the unsatisfying end to the "Ill-advised Curiosity" story, Sondra did as asked, but stormed out of the office immediately thereafter and headed home without turning the Resend Antique off.

Meanwhile, across the city in an underground bunker-like office, a small red light was flashing on a large computer monitor. It was the office of the Central Computer Communications Security Intelligence Agency which had been engaged to battle a rash of computer hacker attacks on the networks and systems of the domestic revenue department.

The attacks began in volume two months earlier. It was shortly after "The Case of the Ill-advised Curiosity – Public Report of Wrongdoing 001" was posted on the department's website, and security investigators soon established a correlation between the internet addresses of computers hacking into the systems and the addresses of computers that had spent more than four minutes on this particular web page. For this reason, the computer security agency was monitoring the use of and access to this website and was following each user in the days that followed.

A large man with a coffee in his hand watching the monitor yelled to his supervisor "Come here quick! Looks like we got a live one."

CHAPTER IX

THE IMPORTANT SCRUTINEY WITH WHICH THE LAWYER AND THE IT EXPERT REVIEWED THE COMPUTER FILES OF DON QUINCY

It did not take long for the technical staff at the Central Computer Communications Security Intelligence Agency to recognize that there was something odd about the computer workstation that had accessed and dwelled so long upon the revenue department's Pillory Page about the Ill-advised Curiosity and to conclude that the situation should be investigated further.

The computer was, due to Don Quincy's multiple Advisory Board linkages as well as Sondra's more recent connections to management email lists and calendars, extremely active and was the intersection of considerable government electronic information traffic.

Enchantingly, the computer was not creating proportionate demand on the central storage systems. This was because Sondra Pantolini had set up an automatic process to archive all of Don's emails, memos, and other messages on the hard drive of the Resend Antique.

The computer security experts were not immediately able to identify the physical location of Don Quincy's computer because the government property records for the old piece of equipment had long ago gone missing. But a particularly shrewd investigator cracked this problem through the bold technique of sending an email to the computer, and thus to Sondra and Don, asking "What's your office room number and building?"

Don's Out-of-Office Email Message and electronic "Manager-of-the-Secretariat" signature block supplied the answer. With this information, the government security agents were ready to seize the computer and search its files for sensitive information, for evidence of security breaches, and, for separate reasons, for any humorous video clips. First, they needed legal authority to act and had to call the Department of Justice and Righteousness for legal and ethical advice. The Information Technology SWAT team members did not like what they were told.

The government lawyer advised them that because of the specific wording of the department of commerce policy on privacy, all emails and files on employee laptops and computers were considered to be the private information of the individual employee unless the contents could be shown to be public information. The precise words in the policy were "Information contained in databases and records of the department are presumed to be in the public interest and to be government property except when they are presumed to contain the private information of individuals which will be the case when public or private information is in the control of individuals who have or may have private and public information holdings."

The Information Technology SWAT team had encountered such legal hurdles before, and for this reason, they knew the loopholes in the system. Even though they were not allowed to open and read Don's emails and electronic files, they could seize computer equipment as government property, and they could read and even delete anything that was on a computer screen that did not require the deliberate act of opening files and snooping around in them. This meant that if they could get into Don Quincy's office when his computer was on, they could review file names, delete suspicious ones and, if necessary, take Resend Antique and put her in storage to take her out of action.

With little effort, the team was able to confirm that Don and Sondra would be out of the office the next day, taking part in the important day-long interdepartmental working group meeting. The Justice and Righteousness lawyer conceded to plans to send an IT SWAT team member to the office the next day on the condition that they not enter Don's office unless the part-time cleaning staff or otherwise fully authorized personnel with master keys opened the door for them and on the condition that the lawyer himself accompany the SWAT team member in order to oversee the examination of computer files.

The next day the lawyer and the IT specialist arrived at the office of the Manager of the Secretariat to the Sector-specific Programs Advisory Board at 7 AM. Sometime before noon, the department's cleaning lady arrived and opened the door. The two men, sharing their business cards and building pass identification, explained to the woman that they too were fully authorized cleaners and were there to clean Don's computer. They were prepared to merely seize it and replace the computer with a similar one, but they were delighted to find it still turned on and illuminated with the file directory open.

The lawyer and the IT specialist looked at each other with smiles and asked the cleaning lady to return in a few hours to finish her cleaning tasks as they would be working in the office for a while. She agreed, and the two men started reading out each file name one-by-one in succession with the object of identifying and deleting files that might contain sensitive or particularly important information that should not be left in the possession of a government employee who may have been corrupted by exposure to the website report of the Ill-advised Curiosity.

They could see that over one hundred thousand files on government policies and management issues sat in Don Quincy's computer archives. They had to act fast and to be focused.

Beginning at the earliest entry and working toward the most recent, the IT specialist started reading out the file subject names with the one entitled "Government-wide Alignment and Integration Strategy."

"I know this announcement," said the lawyer. "I received it too, and it is the policy statement from which all other management directives and announcements have been derived in all the years since."

"Perhaps, we should leave it in his computer," said the IT specialist. "Cause it's an authoritative document, it might be the one that the user of this computer references most often."

The lawyer accepted this suggestion thinking that if it was true, the document's absence would be noted by the computer's owner, and to limit his or her suspicions, it might be better to delete less meaningful and less important documents. They left the file alone and moved on.

After having spared this file, they deleted the next five to keep their exercise in balance and to ensure that any future audit or review of their preliminary investigation exercise would not find them too lax in their decisions this day. They fell upon a series of emails from a manager in the department of citizen health and citizen wellness, which seemed to be identical since the Subject lines were precisely the same. They were identical because Don received multiple copies being, as he was, a named correspondent on so many management mailing lists. The IT specialist was about to delete all of these emails save one on this assumption, but he was stopped by the lawyer.

"The manager who wrote those emails is a former colleague of mine whom I know well," said the lawyer. "He has always been quite polite, helpful, and considerate, and I couldn't live with myself if we were to do him the insult of a mass deletion."

So, the multiple, duplicate files were left intact.

"How many have we deleted thus far?" asked the lawyer.

"Uh, uh, I think five or so," answered the IT specialist. "How about we delete a bunch of these next files since they are basically repeats of the same thing because people have talked back and forth about their lunch plans copying everyone every time they talk back and forth and attaching all previous messages ?"

The lawyer was unconvinced.

"We'll look foolish if we do so," said the wise and thoughtful lawyer. "Because if we were to deem one of these emails to be acceptable and thus spared deletion, how could we argue that other emails with similar information were not?"

The IT specialist, recognizing that they still had well over ninety-nine thousand emails left to examine, asked if they could not just delete all emails received before a specific date: essentially all of the old and potentially irrelevant emails. The lawyer discounted the unsophisticated proposal of the simple IT man.

"If the user of this computer has kept these emails in his archives for many years without deletion, it must be because they are important and valued by him, and he will notice their absence," said the lawyer. "We have to respect the experience and wisdom of the potentially corrupt and dishonorable person using this device as a guide to our strategy. Delete only half of them!"

So the process unfolded for the next three hours. After thoughtful debate and discussion, some emails were saved because of the quality of the Subject line or presumptions about the quality of the writing style and the intention. For the most part, this activity continued for no more than fifteen minutes at a time before the two men mutually agreed to delete thousands of emails capriciously in order to maintain a respectable decision-making pace and to demonstrate courage to themselves and future investigations of this investigation.

Suddenly, they were startled, interrupted, and drawn from their work by the voice of a young woman standing at the office door.

"Hey, who are you two creeps and what are you doing in my uncle's office?" said Don Quincy's niece who was still working in embarrassment and misery in the department's accounts payable branch and still had not found a job elsewhere. "Why are you looking at his computer?"

The two men explained that they were just doing maintenance work on Don Quincy's computer and, in a reactive effort to sound authentic, they said that his computer seemed to be jammed by emails, announcements, and electronic directives linked to public management. The young woman immediately understood.

"This makes sense," she said to the two men. "His head seems jammed with government management policy talk, and it is ruining him – Can I help you weed out these evil messages and soul-killing files ?"

The lawyer and the IT specialist hesitated at first, but then they thought that there could be a legal and administrative benefit down the road to having a next of kin implicated in their enterprise and to have a family member's implicit consent to the acts that their work entailed.

The review of Don Quincy's emails continued in this fashion for the rest of the day. At one point, the lawyer suggested that all of the larger files should be preserved as they were likely to contain information that was important to the user and as their deletion would most likely raise suspicion and privacy complaints. Later, the lawyer said they should delete all large files as these were those most likely to contain important and sensitive government information, the protection of which was their primary concern.

For the most part, Don Quincy's niece sat in silence. She spoke up, however, when the investigators arrived at a string of archived emails relating to treatments for manhood dysfunction. At this point, she pleaded with the lawyer and IT specialist to delete all these emails. Harkening back to the odd and uncomfortable wedding shower with her co-workers, the young woman imagined how much worse the encounter would have been had her uncle been receiving pharmaceutical treatments of the kind promoted in these vile email messages.

Finally, the men completed their review of the one hundred thousand public policy and public management emails in the Resend Antique's archives and packed up to leave the office.

Once again not wanting to raise suspicions, they resolved to leave the computer on just as they found it when the cleaning lady let them into the office that morning. At this point, she returned saying that it would soon be time to go home and that she had to clean Don Quincy's office now.

The two men thanked Don's niece for her assistance and bade her keep the file deletion work secret, and the three of them left the office.

The cleaning lady, an expert in online gambling, noticed while dusting the desk and its contents that the computer was still on and clicked the mouse to log-off and shut it down for the day.

In this process, she was greeted with a prompt seeking a confirmation: "Do you want to delete all of these files or restore ?"

Not knowing any reason to do otherwise and aware that she was in an important manager's office, she selected the cautious option and logged off.

CHAPTER X

THE UNFORTUNATE YET HAPPY FAILURE OF THE STORIES OF SUCCESS

As the computer security team had anticipated, Don and Sondra were occupied all day long at a special meeting in another government building in the center part of the city. Don Quincy had been invited to the meeting through the interdepartmental mailing list of managers in government agencies concerned with industrial strategies, regional development, economic policy, and astrophysics.

Managers and their senior staff were being asked to join a special working group on the development of "success stories" that would be used in some unspecified way to illustrate the good works of the collective. This is the only information Don and others invited to the meeting had been provided in advance; but it was enough to suggest the backdrop of an important pan-government concern, and Don Quincy thought it best to bring Sondra and her Dapple along to record his interventions and encounters.

After passing through a labyrinth of security desks, hidden elevators, and illogical room numbering, Don and Sondra found the meeting room and entered. A sad and tired looking older man sat at the head of a long, oval boardroom table. He was fumbling with papers and did not look up when they entered, nor did he say a word as the room filled up with other people.

When the meeting finally started, the man began the discussion without any introduction or explanatory description of the initiative almost as if it was already well understood by all in attendance. Don was confused and posed what he felt to be an obvious question.

"Excuse me, Sir Chairperson, could you tell us how you intend to use the products of our labors – these success stories," Don asked, recalling that clarity and engagement were fundamental to the effective execution and management of any government program.

The man seemed offended by the question and looking over his reading glasses, he said to Don and the rest of the room in a disdainful way "Our government leaders will use them strategically."

"Strategically!" This was all Don needed to hear. He made no further comment and quietly resolved to be an active and committed member of this vital exercise of national import and dutiful service to Madame Toolemonde.

The reading-glass-wearing, tired-looking man went on to set out the working group's action plan. He said that they and other government managers were being invited to propose their success stories for possible inclusion in a government-wide portfolio, that each success story had to include substantiating econometric data, testimonials from at least ten non-government stakeholders, descriptions of benefits to the economy, environmental protection, human health, and the country's international status, and a summary section of no more than four bullet speaking points, and that each success story would be limited to one page. The Chairperson said that this group would reunite every Monday morning in the same room at 9 AM until further notice. He said that the working group would be divided into three sub-groups to develop plans to address specific issues, but he was not sure what those issues might be save one: "Fonts."

Don Quincy thrust up his hand and volunteered to chair the "Federal Success Story Working Group Sub-Group on Fonts," announcing that his sub-group would meet every weekday except Mondays and said that he would hold his first meeting at the next-to-the-second-floor-elevator meeting room in the department of commerce the following day. The chair said the Font Subgroup would have a budget for focus-group testing and research and development if required.

The next Monday, Don reported on the lively debates at the Fonts Subgroup meetings. He told the larger gathering that his sub-group had yet to tackle the question of font type as they were entangled in the thorny and controversial issue of font size. The Subgroup, he said, had divided into two entrenched factions: those who advocated for a very small font size to facilitate the inclusion of more detailed information in the one-page success story briefing notes, and a second group which felt that this approach would be seen for what it was – an evasion of terseness and an assault on the potential use of the bulleted speaking points. Sondra watched Don aghast with her mouth opened wide as she never knew him to lie so vigorously before. He may have been subconsciously trying to cover for his slipshod colleagues and the lack of any outside attendance at any of his subgroup meetings. But to Don's mind, he was not being untruthful as he never said how many people attended his meetings and was honestly reporting on the font-related debate and dialogue that had been occupying his own mind during those otherwise quiet sessions in semi-solitude with Sondra and her laptop.

Any awkwardness Don may have felt about the modest progress in addressing the font issue was soon erased when he proved to be the first and only manager to table a completed "success story" at that second meeting. Other managers explained their delays by describing the need to have their success stories identified and analyzed by outside consultants; some said that the success story initiative had ignited acrimonious disputes within their departments as branches and divisions feared being overlooked or slighted; still others said that their success stories were stalled in the many layers of approval required before their department's successes could be shared within the government.

With the autonomy of his role in the secretariat of a now non-existent Advisory Board, Don did not have to deal with any of these administrative rituals and was able to write, edit, review, comment on, and approve his success story himself. He was also empowered with ready success story material: the certificate-winning initiative to reduce the costs of operating the Advisory Board which had been celebrated by three federal departments and which had brought special recognition to the senior management of his own. He was also well-equipped to meet the requirements of the success story process because his Advisory Board network connected him to testimonials and the econometric data of activities across many government programs. He managed, with Sondra's help, to squeeze it all into the one-page format, but marked "draft" on the document to acknowledge the unresolved font question.

The sad and tired chair of the working group was pleased to have something to show for the exercise, happily accepted Don Quincy's success story, and added it to his file.

As the weeks passed, attendance at the weekly working group meetings dwindled. Sometimes only Don, Sondra, and someone sitting in for the Chair were there to discuss and review progress. Each week an urgent email message was sent out to the members of the group reminding them to complete their success stories. And each week more names were added to the mailing list which became an ever widening circle and effort to broaden the scope of the government successes to be gathered and possibly, someday, communicated. One day Don noticed the names of his niece and his cleaning lady on the email list as well as many non-government addresses. The working group was encouraged to mine their contacts inside and outside government for story ideas and leads.

One Monday morning, many months after the inauguration of the project, Don and Sondra arrived to find the success story boardroom packed with many new people, a glum-looking chair, and two men and a woman all dressed in dark suits standing behind him. The chairperson explained, for those who were not already aware, that everyone was directed to attend this meeting because there had been a serious breach of security. Email messages and documentation related to the working group's activities had been leaked to the media, and that morning, the front-page of the city's major daily newspaper carried a detailed story about the government's drive to collect success stories that would show its programs in a positive light and highlight its most effective services. The newspaper speculated that the material was being gathered to arm a targeted communications and political messaging campaign to support the implementation of a new national economic strategy.

Sidebar stories about the possible elements of the economic strategy and their impact on varied industrial sectors and regions of the country were printed in the following pages and the Business section of the paper. Don Quincy Bickle and the story of the cost-effectiveness model offered by the Advisory Board on Sector-specific programs were cited in every story to illustrate the government success story initiative. Don's one-page success story was, in fact, printed in its entirety on the newspaper's website with the link to it mentioned in the paper.

The Chair announced that the Working Group was being disbanded, that documentation not required for retention by the freedom of information legislation would be destroyed, and that the members of the working group should not have any further contact with each other until further notice, which would come from someone outside the group. He said that he was personally appalled and disgusted that someone within the government would act deliberately to threaten its operations by willfully sharing information about its successes and its effectiveness with the public and without authority.

The leak of government successes to the media disrupted operations in many departments and agencies, and the follow-up was directed to the Central Computer Communications Security Intelligence Agency for investigation. For this special investigation, investigators focused on the electronic systems, codes, and network hardware involved. The IT specialist, who had, with the government lawyer, reviewed the archived emails in Don Quincy's office months earlier, was aware of the success story investigation because it was big news in his agency. He was not, however, directly involved in it. Perhaps, because of this combination of interest and disassociation, the IT specialist had the luxury of reading the actual contents of the leaked information and the media coverage, and he immediately spotted patterns and words that raised a suspicion. They were, of course, the name "Don Quincy Bickle" and the job title on the name plaque by the office that held that awful management-policy riddled computer.

The IT specialist immediately contacted his superior and shared his suspicion. His manager laughed and told him to keep the suggestion to himself, lest he be ridiculed.

"That guy's a superstar," the IT manager said. "He is one of the top performing managers in the government and recognized for his integrity and honesty; you would get hooted out of the shop if anyone on the investigation team ever heard you saying such a thing."

The IT specialist went back to work and forgot about the issue.

By this time, Don Quincy's name and reputation for management excellence were widely known inside and outside the government. The newspaper story on success stories had been subsequently shared over newswire services and rewritten for television, radio, and many other types of media. The online text of the Advisory Board cost-cutting Success Story was easily clipped and pasted into wiki sites, into blogs, and into government reports.

The media coverage, social networking, and other communications activity not only raised the profile of the department of commerce, but also reflected positively on the work of other government agencies, particularly those embraced by the founding Sector-specific programs that constituted the original Advisory Board portfolio. Many of them took steps to promote their association with the Advisory Board, its successes, and Don Quincy in their own publications and websites.

Discussion of the unprecedented public interest in the commerce department's work soon became the focus of all meetings of its senior management, which was seized with finding ways to reinforce the association with success and excellence. Many suggested that Don Quincy should be celebrated with a special award at a public event. Others noted, however, that his success was already marked by the awarding of a certificate, and it would be inappropriate to award an award to a public servant effectively for having been awarded an award previously. Other members of the management team noted that this had been done many times before.

This debate was resolved by a compromise proposal to establish a brand new award and to do so in Don Quincy's honor such that his example would inspire others to pursue excellence in government service.

Because it was the department's policy to celebrate teamwork, the contributions of all employees, and common values, it was resolved that Don Quincy's assistant should also be included in this special recognition in some way. For this reason, Sondra Pantolini was given the honor of contacting an engraver, ordering the award plaque, and arranging for its delivery.

It was thus that the commerce department Prize for outstanding alignment, integration and strategic excellence in government management became marked and named for "Don Quincy de la Mangement".

The End of Part I

PART II

CHAPTER XI

OF THE DISTURBING CONVERSATION THAT PASSED BETWEEN DON QUINCY, SONDRA PANTOLINI AND "THE PROFESSOR"

"Turkeys," the well-dressed elderly man said in an ominous manner. "My uncle used to own turkeys; thousands of them."

Senior departmental policy advisor Tom Noseworthy liked to gossip, to chat, and to talk: always with awe-inspiring irrelevancy and near limitless capacities for the tangential. His digressions were of minor import, but were always encircled by the air of expectation and pursued with the raw presumption of an attentive audience that was genuinely seeking to listen and learn. For this reason, Tom's colleagues in the department called him "the Professor."

Don Quincy Bickle and his loyal assistant Sondra Pantolini had, to this point, believed themselves to be amidst a discussion of public management practices and the repercussions and reperfusions of Don's great and glorious Success Story adventure.

"Yep, turkeys," the Professor repeated. "I'll never get over that; I'm sure they will follow my spirit into the darkness of my grave."

It was perhaps inevitable that even the solitude-loving Sondra would find herself engaged in conversation with the omnipresent, ever talkative, and sociable Professor. The chance had arrived at the door of the women's lavatory when lightened Sondra's exuberant exit intercepted the distracted Professor's erroneous entrance thereby saving him an episode of unwelcome awkwardness and earning his gratitude. He bowed, thanked Sondra, and asked her name and her position within the department.

Upon learning of her association with the celebrated "Don Quincy de la Mangement" of outstanding alignment and integration fame, the Professor shared some disturbing information that Sondra carried back to her venerated manager-at-large, and she urged Don to summon the Professor to their shared office for what Don immediately recognized to be best recorded in his desk-top calendar as "a formal debrief."

Noseworthy had told Sondra that the whole department, nay, the whole government, knew about her boss and his adventures.

"The creation of the 'Don Quincy de la Mangement' special recognition has been celebrated with enthusiasm by the youngster who is now head of communications," Noseworthy explained, noting that the young man had hired a team of full-time text messaging experts from his high school for the Don Quincy award promotion project. "Some say that the boy credits your manager with his current situation and high salary."

The scuttlebutt generated by the award and its publicity drew out all of Don Quincy's adventures and strung them together into fully fledged government folklore as the women in accounts payable conversed with the business-card-plaque-ordering shop, as investigators in the Central Computer Communications Security Intelligence Agency mused about the still unsolved leak of government successes to the media, and as officials in offices across the federal system sought occasion to war-story about valorous past encounters with the acumen of the now celebrated manager-at-large.

"Your boss's adventures with the offshore wind farm project are so widely known and recognized within the federal system that they have become the allegory for the bash, imaginative, and bold," Noseworthy told Sondra during that first encounter outside the women's washroom. "Anytime, someone suggests a new idea or takes any kind of chance, they are admonished to not go critiquing at windmills."

None of this concerned Sondra much until the Professor lowered his voice and whispered his apprehension that malevolent forces were at work and, he feared, they would ultimately isolate the Office of the Manager of the Secretariat to the Sector-Specific Programs Advisory Board. "Isolate" was not a word Sondra used often in any language, but she could tell from the elderly policy advisor's deportment and next comment that this was someone that Mr. Don Quincy should hear from first hand.

"Fear this department, my dear," the man known as the Professor cautioned. "It is the swamp where the toxic sludge of cynicism floats to the top."

On this day, a few weeks later, Tom Noseworthy was sitting in that very office on Sondra's chair as she stood behind the desk with her manager listening as their guest described the elaborate and intricate process unfolding around them. The Professor explained that managers across the government had been steadily taking measures to distance themselves from Don Quincy and to sever any electronic connections with him. He was being deleted from group emails, from the lists of regular invitees to managerial meetings, and even from the catalog of managers tagged for receipt of routine policy and program announcements.

"They're jealous of Mr. Don Quincy," said an agitated and anxious Sondra. "And they try to make him look bad."

Don seemed less concerned and, smiling to himself, bade the man to continue.

"Well, maybe in some cases," the Professor said. "But more often, it's just his reputation; it scares them."

Noseworthy explained that because the Don Quincy de la Mangement award and arising fame celebrated the notable and commendable conquest of expenditures by the Office of the Secretariat for the Sector-Specific Programs Advisory Board, Don had acquired the status of a cost-cutting professional: "a favored government hatchet man." No one wanted to fall under his scrutiny or accidentally invite his assessment of their programs, services, and email correspondence.

At the same time and as previously described to Sondra, the Professor noted that Don's critique adventure with the windmill project had branded him as a truly creative, daring, and innovative manager, a true leader, and someone who was ready to risk all for the greater public good. He was, therefore, seen as someone to be avoided at all costs.

While the Professor's yarn was the first time Don Quincy had heard of these concerns and the activities serving to segregate him and sever his office from the body of government, it all made sense. In the months since the happy and fortunate failure of the Success Story exercise, Don had noticed a steady reduction in the traffic into his email inbox and the complete absence of further invitations to participate in managerial projects and committees.

Now, the diminishment of his exposure to government messaging was reversing the anesthetizing mental effects of his years of overexposure, and he had started to sense the cheese of his mind firming up, curdling new thoughts, and separating out the old.

Freed from interdepartmental updates and issues, he felt less pressure to read the daily news for treats that could be neatly tied to the policy concerns of the day, and he stopped buying a paper on the way to work. Instead, he dropped by the newsstand on the way home at night to pick up a copy of the Literary Review or an issue of Current Essays and Criticism. He felt a greater need to learn about art, music, poetry, and society, and he thought and thought about all that was elegant and beautiful in life and the quest to contribute to it.

Now, during working hours, in his office on the tenth floor by the elevator, instead of spending his days trying to stay afloat on a whirling flow of new policies, processes, and pronouncements, he had time to reflect, to look back, and to mine the mountain of information he already had on his files. In doing so, Don began to recognize patterns in past decisions and practices, and this caused him to question and challenge the conventions and to doubt what he had previously accepted without pause.

Perhaps, he thought, it may be possible to think it just possible, that just maybe the best government programs were not necessarily those that devoted most of their time, resources, and effort to satisfying the accounting and reporting requirements of external reviews. It also occurred to his emerging-from-the-mire mind that perhaps the best service delivery system might not be an alternative service delivery system that is delivered in an alternative format simply because it was an alternative to what existed before. Perhaps, Don Quincy postulated, decisions should be based on what is best in the circumstances and not what best fits a framework prescribed in abstraction.

This thinking made him feel a little uncomfortable at times, but also more motivated and definitely more human.

It was within this mental milieu that Don Quincy accepted, in sanguinity, the inside intelligence proffered by the Professor.

"I appreciate your concern and the trouble you have taken to come to our office today," Don Quincy said to his guest. "But I believe that overall your distress is unfounded as we are developing our own initiatives and intend to do our best to contribute to the greater good, independent of the circumstances and without the constraint of the agendas and anxieties of others."

It was at this point that the Professor reverted to his "Turkeys" digression. He explained that as a boy he was required to spend his summers working on his uncle's turkey farm, cleaning the overcrowded barns, feeding thousands of birds, packing them into crates, and unloading them at the processing plant down the road. The heat and stench of the barns, the blood and gizzards of the plant, and the weight of the bags of grain would have made for long and miserable days, but, the Professor told Don, none of this registered as the worst part of the job.

"Every once in a while, my uncle would want to single out one of the birds for special food or antibiotics if it seemed different from the others," said Noseworthy. "But all the birds looked the same to me: so he would get me to put a shiny red ribbon around the special bird's neck as a kind of decoration."

Don Quincy and Sondra could not help notice that the formerly confident and assured policy advisor now shivered and looked away.

"Without exception, every time, the other turkeys would isolate the ribboned bird, attack it en masse, and peck it to death" said the now weeping man. "I begged my uncle to stop making me hand out these horrible ribbons and to not single out any one of them for special recognition, but he wouldn't listen, he wouldn't stop."

Sondra had warned her manager that the Professor was prone to extraneous anecdotal digression; and so, recognizing that the turkey-pecking story had to run its course, Don Quincy abandoned hope of ever bringing the conversation back to the bona fide subject of conversation, which was, of course, the outstanding integration and alignment award, government emails, and meeting invitations. Don thus waited for the Professor to pause and take a breath and then suggested they conclude the discussion.

"Well, um, ah, that was a quite remarkable and instructive tale, Sir Professor," said Don Quincy directing his quivering, beside-the-point guest to the door. "I have to return to my schedule now and wish you a good day."

Sondra Pantolini woke up at 2:00 AM that night perspiring, but with a chill. The images of her and Don covered in feathers, running a gauntlet were still lingering in the back of her head as her flickering eyes searched the dark void around her bed.

CHAPTER XII

OF THE SHREWD AND DROLL CONVERSATION THAT PASSED BETWEEN SONDRA PANTOLINI AND HER NEW OLD DIRECTOR AND OTHER MATTERS WORTHY OF BEING DULY RECORDED

The author of this book, having attended most closely in person to the adventures of Don Quincy Bickle, had to rely upon cast-off information from others in order to write this Chapter, which preoccupies itself with the good and solo works of Sondra Pantolini. This portion of the story is untrustworthy as a result and does seem apocryphal because in it Sondra acquits herself in a style unlike what might have been expected from her shyness, inexperience, and disinterest in all things of relevance to her work.

Yet I am compelled to duly record it and to tell you what was reported to me. This being that Sondra was not a vessel overflowing with glee in her nightmare-riddled days following the disturbing turkey session with the Professor. The notion that the whole world - even the whole government - feared her manager and was seeking to distance itself from him was not a blissful thought. Sondra might very well have contemplated leaving Don Quincy and returning to her old real job in the department, but this option was no longer open to her.

Just two weeks earlier, between her bathroom encounter with the Professor and his elaborate "debrief" in Don's office, Sondra had been summoned to a meeting with the department's Director of Planning Information and Data. Her old boss, the kindly man who had arranged her special assignment as Don's assistant, had accepted an offer under the government's new "Extremely Early Retirement Incentive (E2-RI) program" and was gone. His replacement, a much younger man from another department, was now engaged in the compulsory inventory and reversal of recent predecessor management decisions and was merrily attending to them in succession. One decision that the younger man was very anxious to repeal was Sondra's special assignment.

"Why am I paying your salary when you spend all of your time working for another manager," the young man asked Sondra as she entered his office. "This is crazy. We are too busy, probably, maybe, I'm sure, to justify this stuff."

Sondra, whose work with Don Quincy had equipped her nicely to face the unexpected and indecorous, softly explained that the assignment was intended as a personal development measure and that she had every expectation that her job position would be reclassified upwards as a result of her new capacities in strategy, integration and alignment.

The new director became even more irritated.

"What if this hot shot Don Quincy guy gets you boosted two or three more levels up – what if he makes you a manager too?" the man scolded. "Where am I going to get the money to pay for the salary increases, bonuses, and all of your international travel – you'll probably need a clothing allowance too?"

Sondra, sensing that this man might purposely destabilize her more-pay-for-same-or-less-work career ambitions, tried her best to answer saying "the gubermont, maybe ?"

"The government is broke," said the manager. "Besides, the taxpayers don't want public servants to develop their skills and learn new things because it makes them more valuable and more valuable employees are more expensive!!"

Sondra, starting to slip into old patterns, looked down and rested her chin on her chest.

"I suppose if I turn down your request to continue on this assignment, I can expect you to make my life miserable when your fancy friend, this Bickle guy, uses his connections to get you appointed as head of the whole department."

"I promise, Mr. new Director, to not become head of the whole department," said Sondra. "Not right away anyway."

"I am not sure I can trust you," said the Director seeking to regain the upper hand in the exchange. "You haven't ever told me the truth before."

"I haven't ever spoken to you before, Sir," said Sondra softly.

"And that's the point!," he said.

"What point, Sir ?" Sondra Pantolini replied.

"Ah hah !," he said. "I got you."

Their shrewd conversation continued along these lines for a few more minutes as Sondra's contributions gradually drew in a few foreign words and phrases. Then, the vibrating sound of stringy catgut filled out her sentences as tears welled in the corners of her eyes.

The earsplitting, high pitched mix of languages, tears, and tuning instruments overtook the entire conversation. The director covered his ears as he watched Sondra assume the recognizable circular shape that had so distressed the now early retired, former director.

Pleading with Sondra to regain her composure had never worked over the years, but the new manager was uninformed in this as well as other things associated with his position. He tried several times in vein to convince her to stop making those miserable sounds, eventually capitulating to sign the renewal of Sondra's special assignment to permit him to effectively terminate the discussion and to send her back down the hall and into the care of Don Quincy de la Mangement.

CHAPTER XIII

OF SONDRA'S ADVENTURE WITH THE PEOPLE PUPPETS AND THE EDITOR NAMED CHORIZO

Sondra Pantolini was now faced with the certainty of an extended assignment in the service of the former madman, now very deeply thoughtful manager, Don Quincy Bickle. She could see that the worrying issue of isolation from government messages would not be confronted by the vigorless Don in his new, less ambitious state and that she would have to take the reins and strike at the problem herself.

Recalling the Professor's comment about the young boy now heading the department's communication group, Sondra considered the personal debt that the youth owed to Don Quincy. She thought that the youth might be able to help her in her quest to re-elevate her manager to his former status within the government and set out to find the communications management office in order to petition the boy directly.

Sondra was surprised to find the cubicles leading up to the great and powerful boy's office empty and to find, upon arrival at the end of the long corridor, that his office door was wide open with no provision for the formal reception of visitors. But she was even more shocked by the scene that she witnessed upon entry.

The young head of communications was surrounded by a swarming, coarse, angry mob, and he was flailing back in a furious, violent, and bloody fray.

"Never, never, never, you'll never win," the pinched-faced boy shouted. "You scum are all gonna die, die, die?"

A large television screen on the wall was filled with the grotesque rapidly moving images of figures that seemed more like puppets than humans. A large being dressed in black armor with its back turned to all viewers occupied the middle space and was lashing out in all directions with a lance in one hand and a sword in the other. Both instruments were powered by mighty, muscled arms and were busy knocking down the "puppet people" troops, decapitating some, maiming others, and demolishing all as if they were made from almond paste and paper.

All bodies were fomenting blood, bone, and brilliantly colored intestines. The boy-manager, eyes wide and mouth drooling, was pounding his fists on his computer keyboard and stomping his feet.

"Excuse me, Sir, excuse me," Sondra said repeatedly, finally gaining the young manager's attention when the puppets on the screen took flight and retired to fortifications some distance from the dark and aggressive man in armor.

"Whoa, awesome," said the boy manager turning his head toward his guest. "So, what do you want ?"

Sondra described the anxieties over her manager's situation and reputation within the government, and she said that she had hoped that the head of communications might have some ideas, resources, and connections that could help.

It took a few minutes for the youth to grasp the meaning of Sondra's plea and to understand that the great manager she was referencing was the "goofy guy" in the white suit, who had so aggravated his now disgraced former supervisor. He laughed and said that that he could not think of anything to do to help her out, adding that "I don't know much about what they do around here."

The young man told Sondra what she already knew: that the only thing he had done was to hire a bunch of friends under the summer student program to text message, blog, and twoot but said that was just for talking about "funny stuff" like the creation of the Don Quincy Award not about difficult issues or deliberate communications plans. He concluded the conversation by noting that he was not sure he would want to help anyway.

"If I help you, then I'm going to have to help other people," he explained. "And if I start helping other people, then I'm going to have to stop doing other stuff."

As Sondra turned to leave the office of the new head of communications, she was not sure where she would turn next. Then she noticed, on the boy's office wall, a framed article from the department's executive newsletter *"The Management Medium."* The article celebrated the appointment of the new head of communications, his remarkable rise up the ranks, and his gracious acceptance of "the legal settlement." This was all very impressive, but Sondra focused in on the name in large type and bold on the newsletter masthead: "Sammy Chorizo, Editor in Chief." Here was a person who could make things happen; here was a person who knew how to celebrate a career; here was someone who could help restore Mr. Don Quincy to his former status among managers.

The next morning, the assistant to the Manager of the Secretariat for the Sector-specific Programs Advisory Board, presented herself to the Editor in Chief of the department's bimonthly management newsletter to request that he write and publish a story about her manager, Mr. Don Quincy Bickle, just like the one he had done about the boy whose office she had visited the previous day.

Chorizo was an unusual man and always felt a little special in the context of government communications; his passions were history, organizational structures, and interior design. These interests had been developed by the man in the course of earning his Master's degree in Strategic and Aligned Arts online from a university still awaiting admittance to the Ivy League. He now tried to extract some satisfaction from his drudgery-dripping job by using the newsletter to pursue his personal interests.

Thus, in advising Sondra Pantolini that it was not possible to accede to her request, he explained that the *Management Medium* was completely committed and consumed by a thirty-part series retrospecting the various reorganizations, restructurings, and virtual restructurings that had been visited upon the department over the past half decade, adding that he personally was fully absorbed in deadlines for the upcoming issue on office furniture and stationary.

Sondra, now frantic and desperate, pleaded with Chorizo to reconsider in her habitual format of tears and strange sounds.

Sensing that he would not be freed of her throbbing entreaties anytime soon, he sighed and said, "Well, I guess we could give this to Dip."

CHAPTER XIV

OF THE DELICATE INTERACTIONS THAT PASSED BETWEEN DON QUINCY, SONDRA, AND THE DIPLOMA AND OTHER NOT UNRELATED ENCOUNTERS

The man called "Dip" had joined the commerce department as a communications assistant less than a year earlier, after having worked as a newspaper journalist for around a decade. He had been a "beat reporter" for the country's largest and most successful daily paper, covering crime stories and municipal politics. But the internet and electronic age had hit the newspaper hard and had cut its readership to a third of what it was when the man had been hired. This meant it was still the country's largest and most successful daily newspaper, but broke.

Newsroom staff were laid off daily in a well honed routine that required those being terminated to write up a final news story on their layoffs, to post the stories on the internet, and to create a community e-newsgroup on their specialized subject matter before cleaning out their desks and leaving the building. It was this last-day internet and blogging experience that got the attention of the commerce department's résumé screening team and qualified the man for his job in government communications.

The former reporter thought himself extremely lucky to have found a position in a related field, especially in a government department. It meant a grand pay cheque, near adequate health insurance, and a new challenge. But the work situation was not entirely pleasant. Because his qualifications were based upon experience and practical education, he had a hard time fitting in and finding professional acceptance among the seasoned government communications staff licentiated by university degrees such as the much praised Master's of Strategic and Aligned Arts. He was a holder of a mere College Diploma in Useful Communications, thus inviting the tender appellation "Dip."

Dip was overjoyed by the prospect of once again writing a story that would comprise more than 140 letters and symbols. When he arrived at the Office of the Manager of the Secretariat of the Sector-specific Programs Advisory Board to meet Don Quincy and his assistant to gather information for the profile newsletter story, he was well prepared. Dip had read everything he could get his hands on that related to the Don Quincy Award, had interviewed people throughout the department who knew anything about his adventures, and had worked the social networks, microblogging and macroblogging around the clock. He had drafted about twenty-two thousand words and felt that his article was in essence complete. The meeting with Don and Sondra was arranged to confirm the facts and put the icing of first-hand quotes on top.

The interview went well. Dip, Don, and Sondra found that they liked and admired each other. Sondra spoke glowingly of her experiences working for Don and how much she had learned, had professionally developed, and had become aligned. She asked the reporter specifically to mention her professional development and how it was incongruent with her current job classification level in his story. In the interview, Don provided thoughtful observations on his eventful recent career by speaking passionately and eloquently of the values of strategy, alignment, and integration and the privilege of serving as a manager-at-large. As he did, his enthusiasm and folly were, in unison, resurrected.

Don told the newsletter reporter known as "Dip" that the profession of public management should be regarded as "a science" and one "that comprehends in itself all or most of the sciences in the world." The fervent Manager of the Secretariat noted that "he who professes the profession of professional manager must be a jurist and know the rules of justice, distributive and equitable, in matters financial and human. He must be a theologian, so as to be able to ask subordinates to take direction and act on faith, and he must be a psychologist to have the property of healing mental wounds. Finally, a manager must be an astronomer to know by the stars what direction to follow and path to plot into the future."

Dip was not exactly sure what his interview subject meant by all this, but he was certain that there were enough good quotes in there to finish off the story. He thanked both of his new friends for their time and promised to send them a copy of the newsletter article once it was published.

The reporter known as "Dip" wrote a very comprehensive, flowing account of Don Quincy Bickle's recent career, covering all of the major initiatives and many details worthy of being noted in such a history. He was proud of the piece and, for a moment, felt once again like a true journalist. The feeling did not last.

Citing space limitations in the e-version of the newsletter and the need for more "punch," and, perhaps, throwing his intellectual and fully integrated liberal arts weight around, the Editor Chorizo told Dip that his amateurish story would need a lot of editing and that the Editor and Chief would do it himself. He started by cutting out all of the references to "values," "management being like a science," and anything else that seemed to undermine the worth of Chirizo's own education and qualifications. Then, he went on to squeeze the true sense and meaning out of individual sentences and phrases.

Thus, Dip's poignant description of Don's acquisition and use of his Dad's wine-stained white suit became edited into the terse "His father was a drinker." The intervention and follow-up to the incident involving the photocopy room youth and discourteous supervisor became "Bickle has taken a special interest in sexual deviancy" and so on. And whereas Dip ended his article by noting the affection Don Quincy had for his old "Resend Antique" and Sondra had for her Dapple Associates laptop, the conclusion transformed in Editor Chorizo's hands into unfortunate references to Don's old hard drive and the abrupt concluding statement of "She has a Dapple Ass."

CHAPTER XV

WHICH TREATS MANY MATTERS INVOLVING AN INVITATION TO MEET WITH GREAT LEADERS

The head of the commerce department had a particular manner in management and leadership. He would question his subordinates on any difficult matters or urgent concerns that they brought forward in a peculiar and progressive process of probing. By demanding greater and greater levels of detail and greater and greater specialty with greater and greater intensity, he could eventually cause his subjects to collapse and confess the exhaustion of their knowledge on any particular subject at hand. The point of the exercise was usually lost on all of his staff and any witnesses.

But the conclusion of the process was always the same. The department head would send the chastened underling back to his or her office to do more research with the admonishment to be better prepared before he would ever deign to consider the issue anew. The head of the department called this act "drilling" for information. His name was Duke. His staff called him "the Dentist."

Because of his drilling style, the influential Dentist manager was able to rule authoritatively and with the aura of a powerful commander without ever having to make a difficult decision. Because so many issues were deferred to allow further study, the meetings of the department's executive management team became fully preoccupied with agenda items returning to be considered for the third, fourth, fifth or more time. Eventually, even Duke the Dentist found it all too achingly predictable and tedious.

It was with the dread of another such meeting of his executive team at hand that the lord of the commerce department sought some diversion and actual illumination by inviting Don Quincy Bickle to attend as a special non-executive guest. Don was specifically asked to present the "inside story" on the cost-cutting strategies and experiences that had earned him the celebrated certificate and that had been the foundation of the Don Quincy de la Mangement award. The thought of having Don make a special presentation to his committee occurred to "The Dentist" upon reviewing the latest issue of the department's newsletter *Management Medium*. As a very busy and important man, he was not required to read whole newsletter stories or any other documents that ran over a page in length. Instead, he would be presented with a bi-monthly list of headlines such as the one saying "Don Quincy Award – the Inside Story" that had piqued his interest enough to extend the special invitation, but not quite enough to induce Duke the Dentist to read the whole story.

Don was invited to the meeting personally by the department head, via his personal assistant who spoke to an assistant in the Office of the Secretariat to the executive management team who, in turn, contacted an assistant in the office of the executive responsible for paying the rent on Don's Office, who walked down the hall and spoke directly to Sondra Pantolini in Don's office asking that she tell her boss about the department head's invitation.

In order to tell her manager, Sondra was simply required to turn in her chair as Don was sitting beside her in the shared office, listening to the other assistant speak the great invitation. Still, Sondra repeated it word for word with enthusiasm adding additional detail lauding the skies and praising this sign of good fortune which would surely translate into the long-overdue and overly just reclassification upward of her position within the government. As she repeated the message, Sondra amplified the bare invitation with her personal contention that the head of the department must be a person of great grace, gaiety, and charm.

Don nodded in agreement although he knew that these latter words were of Sondra's creation as he too believed the invitation to present himself before the noble and wise committee of executives was portentous and not something to be slighted with unadorned recitation.

To say that our strategic and aligned manager-at-large regarded the opportunity with gravity would understate the state of his mind in the days leading up to the great occasion. He conducted a detailed review and analysis of his experience in the no-expenditures-on-travel-and-meetings exercise all the while seeking to coax out the patterns and principles that would shed light on practice and find general application within the government.

Once this work was completed, Don turned his head to the act of strategically presenting this information in an integrated and comprehensible manner. Sondra assisted by employing computer graphics tools and images to support what Don intended to convey on pages of paper and on a projected computer screen.

In researching ways to present information in fora such as the executive management team meetings, Don noted repeated references to the power and simplicity of the model "Five Point Plan." The concept had its origins in the auto industry, early 20ᵗʰ century socialism, or some other authoritarian system and was now being applied across organizations in both the public and private sectors. Don was impressed by the Five Point Plan's capacity to engage, mobilize, or placate subordinate masses as well as guide the installation of new computer systems application products.

He was enamored for sure. But stymied. For the use of five points conflicted with his other flicker of the ingenious, which was to remind his audience of their righteous purpose and public service higher values by laying his points out individually on horizontal lines – each line beginning with a large letter that would ultimately and vertically spell out the name "TOOLEMONDE." It was a fantastic and peerless idea, and he spent the rest of the day basking in its warm glow.

But the next day, the idea fell down in its application when Don was unable to think of ten points to make in his presentation to match the ten letters in TOOLEMONDE, and Sondra was having a very difficult time fitting all ten lines on the screen anyway. The five-letter "Toole" was another option; but not a particularly good one. So, Don opted for the hybrid "TOOLE – M."

He still faced the challenge of finding another point to add to his five to make a six-point "TOOLE-M" spelling plan. As he stood staring at the computer screen of five points spelling out "Toole" and an orphan letter "M" awaiting its point, trying at once to concentrate and imagine, Sondra Pantolini, as was her custom, interrupted him with one of her unwelcome, droll, and adolescent comments.

"Mr. Don Quincy, I like all your points, and you spell words very well, but what do you do to Make it happen?"

"Make it happen. Make it happen. Mmmm," said Don to

himself. "I have an idea. Let's have the letter "M" stand for the word "make" and then move it to the top line on the list so that the first point before the five-point plan could be 'Make a Five-Point Plan' turning it into a six-point plan, but one that does not disturb or degrade the unrivaled format of the Five-Point Plan. Enchanting. No?"

"Si, you are enchanted, Mr. Don Quincy," said Sondra.

CHAPTER XVI

WHEREIN IS SHOWN PREPARATION FOR THE FURTHEST AND HIGHEST POINT WHICH THE UNEXAMPLED DON QUINCY COULD REACH

The next day, Don and Sondra unhitched "Resend Antique," placed her along with the Dapple on top of a cart acquired from the department of commerce mailroom and ventured forth on another sally: this time exclusively around the executive floor of the building. Don was intent on sharing his ingenious six-point/five-point "M-Toole" presentation with the members of the department's executive management team as a preparatory underpinning to the imminent big event wherein Duke, the department head himself, would be present and would see it.

In each office, the pair were greeted first with quizzical stares, but this turned to courteous welcomes as each of the busy executive managers became overwhelmed by the sight of Don and Sondra, by the tantalizing image of the two odd and awkward innocents appearing unshielded by an executive sponsor in the "Dentist's Den," and by sinister craving. Each one of the executives had had many turns at the painful end of the department head Dentist's drilling, and each watched in incredulous amazement and edgy

110

anticipation as Don and Sondra searched for wall sockets to plug in their portable-on-a-mailroom-cart computer presentation set. Each time Don presented his "M-Toole Lines" concept using his certificate-winning, non-expenditures-experience to illustrate his Lines, the receiving-end executive spectator would smile thinly, commend his manner of thinking, and wish him well in his first meeting with the department head in back-slapping salutations like "Quincy the Line-Hearted" or "Bickle the department's Line Tamer" while stifling sniffs and snorting sounds.

In the late afternoon, having finished the Line presentation rounds, Don went back to his office and Sondra headed off to find the Mailroom Carter to whom they owed the vehicle that had transported Dapple and Resend Antique around the hallways of the department that day. Sondra was starting to feel ill at ease. She could not quite understand why she had been chilled rather than cheered every time one of the executives smiled during her boss's presentation talks. The sensation was solidified into a block of ice when the Mailroom Carter told her that he had been in the room many times bringing in coffee and cleaning up food when the executive manager team meetings were taking place.

His stories of terrorized managers and the sadistic practice of drilling human beings filled Sondra Pantolini with panic. She returned to the Office of the Manager of the Secretariat to the Sector-specific Programs Advisory Board to find Don tired and asleep. Realizing that her manager was exhausted from a long day on his feet and that he had a very demanding meeting coming up, Sondra opened the door slowly, stepped quietly up to Don's ear, and shrieked: "Mr. Don Quincy ! Mr. Don Quincy! Joo es in big trouble. You will be hurt, you will be drilled. Don't go to meeting."

"Well, Sondra," answered Don Quincy with sarcasm. "If you do not like to be in the audience for such a great failure, as in your opinion my presentation to the executive team committee meeting will be, stay back in our office, and keep yourself safe."

Hearing this, Sondra with tears in her eyes entreated Don Quincy to phone in sick and try to get out of making his presentation to the mean-spirited department head. She gravely measured the prospect of maintaining her distance from the looming tragedy as her manager-at-large had suggested. But when the fateful day arrived, the faithful Sondra Pantolini was at Don Quincy's side as he entered the large board room in advance of the meeting to hook up his old computer and the Dapple with the aid of his true and proper colleague, the Manager of the Secretariat of the Department Executive Team meetings. This man told Don that the most important concern in making any presentations in the room was to be mindful of the head of the table and thus the perspective of the head of the department, the drilling-inclined "Dentist." As the table was perfectly round, Don was befuddled as to the location of the head spot and said so.

"I know! I know where it is," said Sondra with excitement. "I know where the head of the table is."

Don glared at his assistant with every fragment of glaring strength within him. She had been invited to attend the meeting on the stated understanding that she would remain mute and would not risk embarrassing her manager with simple-minded and unsophisticated observations on the high matters related to public management and government leadership of which she knew little. He did not want to discomfit himself with an impromptu admonishment of a subordinate before a colleague secretariat manager, but wished with all of his most virgin and pure soul that she would grow silent. She did not.

"The head of the round table is wherever the head decides to sit," she said with a deep breath and the swell of pride.

Don Quincy and his colleague, the other secretariat manager, smiled and shook their heads nodding to each other as they visibly confirmed their shared impressions of the public management bumpkin assistant.

"It's where all the coffee stains are," said the Manager of the Secretariat to this committee to correct Sondra and to clarify.

Don and Sondra set up their computers and screens, checked the cords, pulled out their papers and then took their places in chairs along the wall at the back of the room.

CHAPTER XVII

THE ABRUPT END OF THE DANGEROUS ADVENTURE OF THE LINES

Don and Sondra waited and waited in the executive meeting room for over two hours.

Finally, executives, managers, and assistants started filing into the room and took up the chairs around and beyond the great round table. The Dentist arrived and sat down banging his coffee cup on the table to start the meeting. The first person to speak as part of the prescribed agenda was a not-so-senior information systems manager. He was attending on behalf of his executive supervisor who had taken an abrupt extended leave on medical authority in order to recuperate from illness induced by the stress of anticipating this presentation. It was to elucidate the hierarchy of the department's database and information management system as it pertains to transaction processing, a subject for which the executive was fully accountable and of which he was generally pleased to be fully ignorant. He knew well how his presentation to the department head would end and feared a drilling like none other.

His replacement subordinate, a professional with many years in the electronic information trenches, was, on the other hand, quite comfortable and acquitted himself quite well for most of the meeting. In fact, he thrived on the drilling process, thinking that for the first time someone in senior management might actually be interested in his work, its challenges, and its rewards. He went on and on in response to every drill down question and went into ever increasing detail, so much so that the Dentist's drilling tactic could not keep ahead of him.

Finally, the department head called the session to a halt saying, "There. I think I have made my point; this man is incapable of thinking strategically or considering the higher level tactical issues with which we have to be concerned in this forum. I fear, Sir, you have wasted a great deal of valuable, executive-salaried time today."

The previously proud fill-in meeting attendee, now crushed and embarrassed, shifted back in his chair and looked down.

Next, the meeting agenda called for a report by the most senior official responsible for the department's financial planning, spending, and saving branch, the man who had labeled Don as "Quincy the Line-hearted" in his office a few days earlier and the one who would have described himself, although he was never asked to describe himself by anyone, as the department's "effective, de facto 2-I/C." He too, like the officially ill absentee information technology accountable executive, had good reason to fear the Dentist's drilling on his subject matter of the day: the incredibly difficult, detailed, and dicey "Departmental Audited Annual Financials – the DAAFs."

But this executive had a strategy: a brilliant and never-before-executed-if-ever-in-fact-previously-contemplated scheme sure to succeed in the situation.

The financials executive had brought his branch's leading expert to the meeting to handle all of the drill down questions. Now, such things had been tried before, but the department head found it all too easy to mock his weak and dependent executives when they needed the advice of an underling to survive the executive team gauntlet. But this time, the executive of the financials had a different approach in mind.

Instead of answering questions himself with the likely need to seek his expert's advice. He instead put the bright young expert front and center at the table and let her answer each question directly, fully, and forcefully. But first, before each and every answer and after each and every question was posed, under the terms of a prior understanding between executive and expert, the senior one would lean over and chatter inaudibly into the young one's ears thereby presenting the impression that it was the executive who was in the know and feeding the answers to the other. This process went on for close to an hour. Question posed by the Dentist; executive leans over in silent chattering mode; young one speaks with knowledge and skill; another question, another pretend whispering consult, another answer. Everyone in the room was impressed by the sound of knowledgeable answers, by the executive gentleman's ingenious ploy, and by the Dentist's bright red throbbing forehead of frustration.

Despite the tension, the ruse might have succeeded had the department head not added one final query: "what do the notes to the financials have to do with the strategic alignment and integration exercise that has yet to be formulated and announced ?"

Now firmly caught in the rhythm of the process, the executive, once again aped the demeanor of an advisor leaning over and chattering once again into the ear of the other and then sitting back, only this time to be horrified as the innocent and open young financial expert spoke the following never-before-uttered-in-this-space words "I ... don't ... know...."

A hush of heart-pounding expectation gushed into and across the room. Duke the Dentist looked up and over his half-lensed glasses with a wide smile of glee. What ensued is too ghastly to describe and perhaps only modestly relevant to the adventures of our most integrated, strategic and aligned hero of this tale.

This long crying, shaking, and screaming episode did, nevertheless, provide Don and a perceptibly unnerved Sondra Pantolini with some additional time to go over their slides and notes for the presentation and to test the room's video projection system for compatibility with the unique multi-Line, individually-labeled-with-a-letter "M-Toole" graphics.

"Now, as our final agenda item, I have invited one of our most respected managers and a leader in government service in the area of spending reduction and the introduction of new non-spending activities, Mr. Don Bickle of the Integration Advisory Board secretariat," the department head said incorrectly, but with a blend of solemnity and pageantry. "I believe Mr. Bickle can teach us a lot about how to reduce our activities and service levels thereby reducing demands on the public, which I would remind you is our ultimate concern."

Don walked up to face the coffee-stained end of the round table, straightened the now frayed remnants of his wedding-shower headpiece, tightened the sash around his white suit, cleared air from his upper entrails, and began.

With his six-point/five-point "M-Toole" slide on the screen at his side, Don Quincy, as if in a trance, began a soliloquy of his personal reflections on the philosophy and theory of public management, acknowledging that his passion for administration was radical although his ideas were founded upon the orthodox. Periodically, he would address the department head directly as "Mr. Dentist" as several of the other executives had advised him to do, and periodically, he flirted with the line between information and instruction, hinting that the department head himself could gain from the refreshment of greater study and thoughtful research in the arena of management science.

Using a supplementary graph, Don explained that he had noted a pattern in public management issues that clearly demonstrated that government managers preferred to work in environments that were "stable" and "desirable," yet there were situations that were "unstable" albeit "desirable," others that were "stable" but "undesirable" and still others, possibly the least preferred that were "unstable" and "undesirable." He added, however, that if a situation is "undesirable," it might, in fact, be better if it was not stable since it would be a situation that one would not want to persist. In his summation, Don drew Lines moving from various stable, unstable, undesirable situations to the desirable and stable one as his model for the essential task of public sector management.

The others in the room might have broken into unbridled laughter were they not at once stunned, shocked, and scared. Those who had not been involved in the preparatory set-up consultations thought Don Quincy to be exceptionally brave if unwise in his daring interactions with the Lines.

"So, if you, Mr. great Dentist, Sir, or anyone else has any questions, I would be prepared to confront them with pleasure," Don said to his audience after thirty minutes of verbal enthusiasm and motion.

Silence. An uncomfortable elongated period of silence.

Then, after about five minutes, the head of the department slowly lifted his gaze from the mobile communications device that had preoccupied his attention throughout the presentation, swallowed, and looked around the room. A flood of overlapping email messages, some from his stock broker, some from a woman he had met on a recent business trip, some from his wife, some from his lawyer, had filled his device and his mind throughout Don's presentation of which he had not heard a word, and now the Dentist was not sure to whom he had sent an email response and with what words.

He called the meeting to an end.

"Well, ah, thank you Quincy," the man said, still distracted by the stream of electronic messages that had held his attention over the previous half hour. "Send that presentation to my office, and we will circulate it to the usual list."

With that, he left the room, and Don and Sondra packed up amidst the ruckus of mumbles and murmurs from the others as they returned to their offices on the building's top floor.

CHAPTER XVIII

OF THE MANAGEMENT OF CRISIS AND SINISTER PLOTS

Within a few days, the office of the head of the department had fairly distributed electronic copies of Don Quincy's Lines Presentation via the Dentist's own email system thereby giving the document an authority and sanction that it would not otherwise have had. Soon, everyone in the department was referencing Duke's "Lines Theory" and management model in meetings on the analysis and discussion of any initiative that sought to reduce spending or to move a situation from varying forms of "undesirable" into the "desirable" zone.

Taking care to always give due credit to the department head, managers at all levels would soon use and cite the technique and slide graphics in meetings with other government managers and eventually with clients and experts beyond the boundaries of the federal government as a whole.

As any political, legal, or financial crisis was deemed to fall within the "undesirable" domain, the Don-Quincy, now department-head, "Lines Management Model" was regularly applied to the process of confronting any crisis. The concept of high public service and the link to Madame Toolemonde slowly faded from replications of the

120

presentation and the model, which eventually became cited simply as the commerce department "M-Tool" and presumed to mean "The Management Tool."

One of the public servants and would-be managers most enchanted by the M-Tool was a university political economy professor working in the government under one of its many, ill-defined, but certain-to-be beneficial-to-all exchange programs. When he returned to the academic world, the man was empowered by actual government employment experience, allowing him to interpret his advanced degrees in economics and politics as adequate enough credentials for research and publishing in the public management field.

His book *"Crisis Management in the Federal Government: Getting to the Desirable,"* was widely read and highly regarded within the analysis-of-what-is-wrong-with-government-from-outside-and-from-a-distance academic circles. Reviewers typically lauded the model for moving to the "desirable," which the academic, former short-term government employee had refined.

But the greatest scholarly praise was reserved for the combination of elegance and practicality embedded in the novel concept of "the Six-Point Plan," soon universally regarded as the next step in public management thinking and a clear advancement on the historic, but perhaps limited "Five-Point Plan" model of classical theory.

Don Quincy Bickle might have been buoyed by these developments and by knowledge of the wide impact his thinking and theories had had, but he was completely absorbed during this period by administrative and clerical demands generated by a completely unanticipated consequence of his renewed notoriety within the department.

This came about due to the personal intervention of the man who would have described himself, if he had ever been asked, as the department's "de facto 2-I/C." This man, the executive so battered in the chattering-into-the-ear-of-his-expert incident, was bitter and increasingly envious of Don Quincy's renewed reputation.

In fact, this executive was among the loudest mutterers and mumblers as that auspicious meeting ended. That very day, he posed aloud to one of his executive colleagues leaving the room the question: "I wonder if Mr. Wonderful, Bickle, has ever had the joy of an audit and special review of his stellar program?"

As the most senior official responsible for the department's financial planning, spending, and saving branch, the executive had easy access to the levers that induced and directed such audits and reviews. It was simple to justify an in-depth examination of Don Quincy's Secretariat operations since they had been touted as the model for others to emulate.

So, what arose from vindictiveness and malice was advanced as a sincere effort to learn best practices.

CHAPTER XIX

OF THE TERRIBLE AUDIT AND REVIEW FRIGHT THAT DON QUINCY ENCOUNTERED IN THE WAKE OF THE PRESENTATION TO THE EXECUTIVE TEAM COMMITTEE

Don and Sondra were concerned, even a little frightened, the day that the energetic audit and review team broke down the door to their office, turned over the filing cabinets, and pried open the drawers to Don's desk.

Despite this tense beginning, Don Quincy grew to like the members of the team, and in the weeks and months of auditing and reviewing that followed, he had many lively and enjoyable conversations with the leader of the audit. Don told the man that he himself had even toyed with the idea of becoming an auditor in his youth and had taken a few college courses including Serial Numbers 101, Advanced Receipts, and Unregistered Transactions.

Having established this kinship, the two discussed the profession of strategic reviewing and auditing at length with particular application to Don's personal capabilities as an administrator and his professional security in the context of the active audit and review.

"I don't know, Bickle, whether you would have the right stuff," said the audit team leader with mild condescension. "Part of the job is pretty straight-forward, but other parts are really, really hard."

He explained that the easy part rested in the fact that strategic reviewers and auditors would either find something or not. If they found something, it would give them lots to talk about in their final report. If they did not find anything, then it would be evidence that the audited party was not keeping comprehensive records and that it could not be shown with certainty that there was no problem.

"The hardest part of the job rests in the primary professional obligation of all auditors and administrative reviewers to craft their final recommendations in a form that calls for the hiring of more auditors and administrators in government," the auditor explained. "It's not always easy because we deal with so many different subjects and different kinds of government programs - it takes some effort and it takes a while to get the knack of turning it all around to that fundamental point of hiring more auditors."

The man told Don that his fallback in the absence of other, more creative ways to advocate more jobs for his profession would be to recommend follow-up audits, reviews, and reports thereby, at the very least, creating more work for his professional kin if not more auditing and reviewing jobs.

The audit team leader confessed that the review of the Office of the Secretariat to the Sector-specific Programs Advisory Board was a challenging project in this context. Normally, the work of the auditors and reviewers was circumscribed by the definition of "materiality." Materiality is the dollar amounts of the transaction or transactions under review that are deemed important to the project and its omission could influence the findings. Sometimes this amount would be as little as $100; other times it could be as much as $ 1 million in government accounting.

But the review of Don Quincy's office was spawned by the desire to understand his success in achieving zero spending, zero transactions, and zero business. Thus, materiality was set at "zero" for this project, and the audit and review team dutifully set out to find documented evidence to attest to the assertion that Don had not spent anything or done anything in the years under review.

The auditors searched every email; they read and impounded every scrap of paper; they went through Don's wallet, and they took the certificate from his wall. But in the end, they could not find any evidence that that showed he had not done anything of a financial nature during the audit years.

Despite a personal fondness for Don and Sondra, the audit team leader had no option, as a disciple of his profession, but to file a scathing report that condemned the lack of records of non-transactions, the frustrating-to-audit-and-review-teams failures in administrative practices, and the apparent general disregard for the rightful interest of the taxpayer in no-cost, non-spending inactivity.

Oh, disaster. Don Quincy Bickle, a man whose greatest aspirations as a manager-at-large rested upon his reputation for professional administration and his chaste commitment to the taxpayer Madame Toolemonde, was crushed.

The day that the audit report was submitted to the head of the department, Don took his copy home with him and placed it on the pillow next to his head as it sought the escape of sleep and dreams.

First, however, he burst, not into tears, but into sighs, an act of delicacy and good breeding that he deemed more worthy of the government manager and leader that, despite the auditors' loss of his wall certificate, he still believed himself to be.

CHAPTER XX

OF HOW THE AWARD AND MANAGEMENT LIFE OF DON QUINCY DE LA MANGEMENT ENDED

Although many weeks had passed, the throbbing sting of the audit report had not lessened, and it was thus that Don Quincy was un-astonished to learn from Sondra one Monday morning that he had been, via the chain of administrative assistants, summoned to appear at Duke the Dentist's office to review the report's findings.

Don invited Sondra and her Dapple laptop to come along with him to the ominous meeting as he believed it proper and just to have his reprimands recorded as well as his celebrations. They sat in the cordial reception area outside the great department head's office for over an hour before finally being asked to enter and sit down.

Duke appeared, as expected, stern and distressed.

"Quincy, you know why you are here," said the man known as the Dentist. "We've got to do something about this audit report; in fact, my deadline for giving a formal written response and taking action is today."

The somber department head manager turned his gaze away from Don and Sondra, and he looked out the window with a rueful face.

"I have been putting this off Bickle, but I know what has to be done," Duke the Dentist said, for the moment showing no interest in his drilling techniques. "You have to know this is one of the most difficult things for a public service manager to do, particularly when it involves someone like you who had seemed to be doing so well."

The moaning sound of stringed instruments being tuned up entered the already tightly strung atmosphere in the room. Don braced himself and thought that the meaning of his long career in government service was coming down to this moment.

"I guess that I have no choice, but to increase your budget and the size of your office," Duke said with resignation and his own burst of sighs.

The stunning pronouncement confused Don and Sondra until the man explained that the post-audit analysis concluded that its essential message to the department was that Don Quincy had not had been assigned adequate financial management and administrative support and that this was the root and the cause of the missing records on his non-expenditures and non-activity. Duke the Dentist concluded by saying that he and his colleagues recognized that the situation could not continue and that they had let Don Quincy down.

"Clearly, we need to hire more auditors and administrators of our own to work in your group in order to better confront the auditors and administrators who are sure to conduct a follow-up review of your office and the debacle of your lack of prior adequate support," said Duke in a best-ever effort at an apologetic tone. "I hope you will find it in your renowned managerial capacities for compassion and understanding to move on from this experience and not let it influence your perspective on government and this department."

Don assured the man that he would and prepared to return to his office where he and Sondra had considerable inactivity to record and add to his files. But first, the department head had one other announcement to make.

"Bickle, I want you to know that we will no longer be handing out the Don Quincy award," said Duke. "It is just too dangerous; if we find some other great program and give the manager the award, then we risk inviting another audit of best practices and more recommendations to hire more auditors and administrators, and I just can't afford it for the time being."

Don was saddened inside, but hid it well and understood the decision.

On the way back to the Office of the Manager of the Secretariat to the Sector-specific Programs Advisory Board, Don and Sondra ran into the Turkey-story Professor, Tom Noseworthy, whom they had not seen for many months. The Professor explained that he had left government service and was just back in the department, in a way, visiting. In fact, he was now the President of a Government Interactions consulting firm and was just renewing old friendships after the completion of his mandatory post-employment purification period.

Don had nothing else on his mind, but the audit, the meeting he had just left, and the cheerless termination of the peerless Don Quincy Award for Excellence in Integration,

Strategic and Aligned Public Service. So, he told the Professor about it.

"Didn't you pay attention to anything I said about Turkeys, Awards, and Government," said Noseworthy. "You don't need the damn things, and you sure as hell don't want one named after you."

The Professor was not big on public service awards.

"In this town, if you stand on a corner long enough, somebody's goin' to give you some damn award," he said. "They throw them around like confetti because they can't do anything else; there's the Treasury Department rules, the union contracts, the paperwork performance reports, and all the foggy sensibilities that prevent government managers from really rewarding people that do a good job. So, we cook up awards, awards, awards."

He then recounted how he personally had been caught in the government award whirlwind. It started early in his career with the receipt of many middle-manager awards from his middle-manager supervisors, then later as a middle manager himself, he received middle manager awards for middle managing.

"It all made me wonder if I had my head screwed on right or not," Noseworthy said. "The one that drove me over the top was the special departmental centennial award for "Short Term Apparent Interest in His or Her Work." My mother was so ashamed, she wept for days."

Noseworthy explained that he wasn't opposed to recognizing people for doing good things, but really wanted Don to look for validation inside and not from the government public management system.

"Everybody is special in their own way, everybody is number one at something, being themselves, and you just have to find that combination of human qualities that makes you who you are and what you are," the man said now fully reverting to his Professor persona. "Even kids are told to be who you are and say what you feel, because those who mind don't matter and those who matter don't mind."

Then he added, "Don, I have always thought that you are, for example, the World's Best Daydreamer – you're like the Michael Jordan or the Gretzky of Daydreamers, and you should be proud."

After he said good-bye to Noseworthy and walked down the hall, Don Bickle, thought about what had been said and found himself looking at life differently. It started with the realization that he may indeed be the World's Best Daydreamer. A flood of memories from his childhood as a daydreamer in school to his personal life as an adult and his career in the public service flowed across his mind showing a clear pattern and permeation of intense and regular daydreaming.

Now, he was daydreaming about daydreaming. His true being could not be any clearer.

The buoyant thought that he might achieve excellence by just being himself without reference to public management processes, administrative practices, and government policies prompted many changes in Don Bickle's routine and life. He put the white suit back in storage and bought new business clothes. He took down the sign from his door, and he cleaned out his files. Within a week, he had given every personal item in his office to his niece, the cleaning lady, and Sondra.

Rather than seeking a reclassification for Sondra Pantolini's job, he helped her, with a glowing reference and attestations to her loyalty, to secure a new job at a higher level working in the office of the information systems manager so embarrassed for his lack of strategic sophistication at the executive team meeting. Don bought Resend Antique from the government computer disposal service and brought her home to rest on his own desk in his study, and he submitted his resignation in order to retire from government service a few years early. The Professor offered Don a job with his consulting firm, and Don accepted on the condition that he would only serve non-government clients.

He did not announce his retirement in any way at his place of work as he knew that the others would think him foolish for having left government service before his pension benefits had been maximized through the venerated combination of years of life and years of service. He knew that others would have also mocked his choice of pastoral life over the vibrancy of government management.

Thinking of his career as a servant of the public, Don was a little wistful, more for what might have been rather than what had been, and wondered if he would be remembered as a man in madness or a man within madness. He soothed himself with words that he had read years before his entry into government: "nothing that is man's can last for ever, but all tends ever downwards from its beginning to its end."

Don Quincy Bickle walked out from the dark shadow of the building that had been his professional home for many decades for the last time and into the sunshine of a warm spring day, thinking himself blessed and entering the boundless. Then, he turned and softly said "Farewell."

- The End

ABOUT THE AUTHOR

Michel D. Cervésasse is a non-existent, imaginary, and fictitious person, maybe even a group of people, or an inanimate entity, who wishes to deny his, her or their true identity for no particular reason other than to be able to use a name that seems more distinguishing, aesthetic, and apt in this circumstance.